Miniature Garden
G U I D E B O O K

for beautiful rock gardens • container plantings • bonsai • garden railways

Nancy Norris

KALMBACH BOOKS

Foreword

The pastime of garden railroading can be traced back around 150 years. At that time, little heed was paid to the miniature landscape or suitable plant material—it was all about the trains. It wasn't until the late 1920s and '30s, when the work of people like Roland Callingham in Great Britain (creator of the wonderful miniature railway, Bekonscot, still open to the public today) and Frank Roberts in New Zealand became widely known, that people began to consider the garden an integral part of an outdoor model railway.

Garden railroading declined after World War II. In the United States it all but died out. In the late 1960s, a new line of trains from Germany, called LGB, rekindled interest around the world. In the United States, garden railroading was viewed as something new and, indeed, the hobby had to start nearly from scratch here. Garden railroading as we know it today in America is only about 40 years old.

Having said this, garden railroading has made evolutionary strides that sometimes defy belief. The work being done by many of its adherents borders on the incredible. What makes it so is, most often, the integration of a well-thought-out railway skillfully integrated into a beautiful scale garden, as you will see in these pages.

I know of many railway gardeners who began the outdoor aspect of their hobby simply as model railroaders. Upon taking up spade and trowel, they discovered the magic of gardening. Many have become excellent—even visionary—gardeners in their own rights, even though most of their gardening knowledge came through their interest in garden railroading. Railway gardening has become a unique pursuit all its own, as broad and deep as the railroad hobby associated with it.

In these pages, Nancy Norris covers miniature gardening thoroughly. She has her own way of approaching the subject, bred of a combination of her many years of experience as a professional gardener, her avid involvement in garden railroading with a genuine interest in things "railroady," and a sense of whimsey. She covers not only the various types of plants, their uses in the context of the railway garden, and their care, but the bigger picture of landscape design and aesthetics. I'm sure you'll learn much from her writings and enjoy the process as you go. This is much more than just a gardening book—it is an open door into the wonderfully unique and quirky world of railway gardening.

—*Marc Horovitz, Editor,* Garden Railways

Kalmbach Books
21027 Crossroads Circle
Waukesha, Wisconsin 53186
www.Kalmbach.com/Books

Published in 2011
15 14 13 12 11   1 2 3 4 5

Manufactured in the United States of America

ISBN: 978-0-89024-777-8

Publisher's Cataloging-In-Publication Data

Norris, Nancy (Nancy M.), 1949-
    Miniature garden guidebook for beautiful rock gardens, container plantings, Bonsai, garden railways / Nancy Norris.

    p. : ill. (chiefly col.) ; cm. -- (Garden railways books)

    ISBN: 978-0-89024-777-8

    1. Railroads--Models--Design and construction--Handbooks, manuals, etc. 2. Gardens, Miniature--Handbooks, manuals, etc. 3. Miniature plants--Handbooks, manuals, etc. 4. Container gardening--Handbooks, manuals, etc. 5. Bonsai--Handbooks, manuals, etc. I. Title.

TF197 .N67 2011
625.19

Contents

For centuries, Asian artists have combined principles of visual beauty with the illusion of scale and the science of cultivating plants gathered from mountainsides. Some families maintain these classic scenes for generations. This tray by an anonymous artist was a floating display on a pool at the San Francisco Conservatory of Flowers. Just two plant species soften the sculpted stones and white sandy 'sea', elegantly telling the story of the mountain island. See Chapter 18 "Low-down groundcovers" and Chapter 19 "Micro-miniature trees and shrubs" for more on these plants.

Introduction

More than 200 miniature gardens, mostly in private garden railways in North America, were researched for this book. In Part 1, a gallery of gardens from a range of geographical locations shows how gardeners designed little green landscapes to fit their native habitat. Every one of them has a story to tell; each displays a distinctly different setting and each designer is unique. Space doesn't permit sharing every railway garden with their fascinating ideas and delightful details, but this book tells you how to find them.

In gardens that were small or large, with four plant species or 40, I looked for examples to tell the story of miniature gardens. I wanted to know how to grow them, where plants would grow, which miniature plants were working best, who these miniature-garden people are, and why they do it.

Why do happy, sane, mature adults (and some kids) cram hundreds of tiny plants into a garden when 10 or 12 large plants will cover the ground? Then they join clubs and visit other scaled down gardens every month. Some seem to enjoy passing on their skills to other club members and opening their yard to the public after spending weeks to get ready. Sometimes these gardeners band together with others of their ilk and they build garden railway layouts at public places. A long list of these public gardens is in the appendix.

Nostalgia for an era gone by is one reason for modeling little villages and extinct railroads. As they get older, seniors want less space to maintain. They move to smaller places, and then find they still have the urge to garden. Miniature gardens afford more design and cultivation time without lifting heavy trees and digging 3' holes for plants. Some families unite to entertain beloved grandchildren and create Disneyesque worlds, just for fun!

Many traditional indoor modelers transitioned into this hobby by expanding their garage or basement model train display into the great outdoors and had no idea what to do with plants. At first they wanted realism in scenery, like the murals painted on their basement walls. With experimentation, they discovered the plants are alive! And grow! Or don't! Part 2 will introduce new gardeners to basic landscape design for miniature scenes, how to care for them and how to keep them small. Many of these former indoor model railroaders surprise themselves to find they enjoy the miniature plant world as much or more than the railroad.

Techies, who like to make things move with electricity, water, and engines, want to dress up their railroads to integrate them into their backyard. On the other extreme is a group of railroad gardeners who love to be engineers—more civil engineers than train

The "growing" art of garden railways involves civil engineering skills to maintain mountainside hardscapes and to run trains on a suitable grade for engines. The combination of dwarf shrubs pruned into trees to shade low groundcovers creates the living scenery that helps to make the buildings and figures come alive. This railway empire represents an early Japanese artists' community visited by tourists via the Osaka & Orient Express. The garden was designed and built by the author for Jim Ditmer, who wanted a garden and theme to display his collection of aged bonsai trees, like the blue atlas cedar, coral bark maple and stone pine on the right. The author trimmed a row of five Seiju dwarf elms for the park at top and a riverside blooming dwarf tea tree on the left.

engineers—and spend months incorporating fancy land masses, bridges and finally exquisite dwarf plants from specialty nurseries, some of which you'll find in the appendix.

What is it about these miniature and dwarf plants that attract so many people? Research shows that these gardeners want to be the rulers of their tiny empires. The ability to create a little living landscape is a compelling reason to stay home and develop amusing scenery, replete with moving trains and water, little figures and scale buildings. Railway emperors and empresses design their little worlds, as they want them, with help from the plant kingdom.

Garden Railways magazine has been leading folks into this hobby and keeping them busy building manageable and modest layouts or elaborately complex scale countrysides since 1984. I've heard it called "the bible." Links to online *GR* articles in the appendix will help you get acquainted with railway gardening, lead you to garden railroad clubs you can join, and get you started on your own projects. Pertinent articles

from my column in *GR* ("Greening your railway") are included in this book along with the contributions of regional gardening reporters, who broaden the scope of the material. It was also through the dedicated folks who host the National Garden Railway Conventions (see links in appendix) that I was able to photograph these gardeners' creations enabling me to share their gardening practices with you.

From all over the world, friends and *GR* readers have sent me photos of their mini-plant projects. They invited me into their gardens and helped me compile the data in the plant charts within Part 3. This hands-on section shows you how to choose very small plants to take on jobs like preventing erosion from ruining trackwork, repelling or inviting the animal kingdom, surviving drought, and creating scale landscapes for structures. I appreciate the expertise of all the gardeners who were thrilled to share their view of this pioneering hobby. With their gracious help we have a window into our wonderful world of miniature gardening.

1

Gallery of miniature gardens

In the Zone 2 foothills of Alberta's Canadian Rockies, the Miens family of train enthusiasts built a ½"-scale (½" = 1') railway under full-scale (1' = 1') Alberta spruce trees, whose seedlings sprout and blend into the forest floor. Native wildflowers mingle with store-bought groundcovers, like the blue creeping speedwell in the foreground. The Miens' leave all little wildflowers and trees until they get "too tall" and then remove them. It works! Details, like matching the yellow ducklings with the marsh-mari-gold flowers draw us in, so we notice the red-blooming saxifrage reflected in the pond.

Welcome to the gallery of miniature gardening. Notice in these images how artists have applied civil engineering skills to a palette of plant, stone and commercial materials of their choice. Each picture has a definite theme. As students of art and ornamental horti-culture, we can identify ways that the many elements fit the backdrop nicely and play on each other to depict a scene from the reaches of the artist's imagi-nation or a place on the map to tell a story. We stick around to search for the surprises created for our enjoy-ment— or possibly just for the artist's amusement.

Nature and its range of habitats will always offer opportunities for each gardener's "canvas," regardless of the inevitable climate restrictions. Let's voyage from the northern cool forests of Canada's Zone 2, to the steamy heat of Hawaii's Zone 11 and visit all the regions in between. (Find your hardi-ness zone in Chapter 2, "Zoning laws for climate compatibility.") While traveling, ask yourself questions. What natural and man-made elements will transform a piece of ground into a last-ing landscape that could take a lifetime to explore, revisit and appreciate? How can I recreate my mind's ideal geo-graphical location within my backyard, which is different from all other yards?

In Alberta's Zone 3 high prairie, where winter Chinook winds alternately heat up and then freeze-dry little plants, Robin and Lucia Edmond learned to stick with only nursery plants that survive their region's winter. Even buildings have to withstand the repeated freezing and thawing that hammers this area every winter, and rabbit-chasing coyotes won't break these buildings. Lucia created a whimsical world from boulder buildings, all artfully painted to fit the scene, like this spherical dwelling for a ceramic elf. His never-mown lawn is the palest blue creeping speedwell (*Veronica repens*, Zones 2-8). To deter rabbits, deer and other invaders, see Chapter 15, "Isolate your garden from nuisance nibblers."

Also in Alberta's Zone 3 high prairie, Verne and Kathleen Clayton took another approach and bought all natives from a local natives nursery for this section of their garden railway. Hiding the fence is a hardwood forest of multi-stemmed tundra dwarf birch (*Betula glandulosa*, Zones 2-9). Prairie Smoke (*Geum triflorum*, Zones 1-8) pokes up its seasonal pink whiskers and the yellow Canada bean (*Thermopsis rhombifolia*, Zones 4-8) is massed to disguise its height. For a scale presentation we look through the strap leaves of blue flag (*Iris giganticaerulea*, Zones 3-10) to see that Kathleen added her own scale touch of a blue boulder building, having taken lessons from Lucia Edmond. See Chapter 4 for ideas on "Massing plants to frame a focal point."

No, this isn't a Christmas scene, it's May 27! Joan and Tony Scheiwiller model the Swiss Alps, their home of origin, in their Big Sky Garden Railway in southern Alberta's Zone 3. Her creeping phlox was in full bloom and easily survived the frosting. Find hardy ground huggers for your zone in Chapter 18, "Low down groundcovers." *Joan Scheiwiller photo*

Maine's Zone 4-5 Acadia National Park provides the ultimate in micro-scale background beauty. Black stud lichens and fields of orange and gray-green lichens cling to Maine's famous pink granite. A micro-moss meadow embeds a crevice shared with an avalanche of white quartz. If all rocks were this interesting, we wouldn't need plants, but we can model ancient cliffs with rocks from the quarry and low, draping plants. Chapter 11, "Cascading plants and the rocks that support them," suggests ways you can build elevation into your garden with natural stone.

Bill and Liana Hewitt used artistic placement to set off this scene on their Southpark and Dogbark Railroad in Massachusetts' Zone 5. Burgundy Japanese maples create a "view break" of the dark area under the deck. In contrast, two bright green dwarf boxwoods shelter the town square. Neutral colored stones blend into the sidewalk, frame the scene, and elevate the layout closer to eye level. Read how gardeners add interest in Chapter 5, "Color me content."

On Rhode Island's Zone 6 coast, Manny and Veronika Neronha integrate their garden railway into the surrounding yard of towering shade trees by blending medium-sized ornamental trees with smaller "scale" trees closer to track and structures. As we tour the layout, new green vistas surprise us at every turn. To show off scenes up front, they trim their spreading junipers to fit the space and represent low hills. Chapter 17 offers 20 dwarf "Junipers to appreciate."

On a mini-mountain garten bahn in Germany's Zone 6-7, sedums of many species clothe the rocks in succulent hardiness. The combination of heat from the sun-baked rocks and the constant draining of water from the hill, makes drought-resistant plants, like succulents, a smart choice for long-lived mini landscaping. Chapter 13 lists "Drought resistant plants and practices to reduce water usage." *Hanna Moog photo*

Danny Saporito has captured a moment in time by incorporating dozens of seedling trees from his native Zone 7 Long Island, New York. Expanses of groundcover edge right up to the stream. We can almost hear the plop of the bobber as the fishing line hits the water. He used a deep part of his yard so that no depth-of-field tricks are needed. Fishermen waving to the D&PRR at the far end of the stream make us believe the story goes on forever. See Chapter 3, "Design your mini garden," for ways to get a scale perspective.

The Quinn Mountain Garden Railroad in the foothills of Washington's Zone 7-8 Cascade Mountains has carved out a little sunshine from the forest to run trains. Bud Quinn built the railroad and Christina Brittain cultivated the scenery from a palette of shade-loving miniature plants. Under a clump of birches, two shockingly white *Cryptomeria japonica* 'Nana Albospica' (Zones 5-7) reflect the white birch bark and light up a maroon distillery. One of the fun things about visiting other gardens is discovering "new" plants to grow. Actually, this variety of dwarf variegated Japanese cedar has been in cultivation since 1868! See Chapter 19, "Micro miniature trees and shrubs," to find 40 cultivars (varieties) of truly miniature trees.

Having the space to spread out in northern California's Zone 9, Don and Marilyn Pickett were able to develop several areas, each with a distinct personality. The Little Creek Ranch, upper left, is watershed to the creek, which fills the pond. To provide some cooling shade for the large shallow body of water, the author carved an island out of feather rock and planted it with bald cypress trees. Pots of parrot's feather (anchored to the rock) oxygenate the water to promote a healthy balance of microorganisms. See Chapter 10, "Aquatics have wet feet," for more on plants for water-features.

Maintaining the fully mature Riggston Central Coast Railroad in coastal California's Zone 9 means getting into it to cut back groundcover and trim trees. Dan Riggs accesses his trains and plants by creating narrow roads from tamped down decomposed granite. Knowing where to put your feet during a busy open house of running trains avoids breaking a foot-high 10-year-old tree or other catastrophes. See Chapter 6, "Easy access into your garden," for more solutions.

Two brothers collaborated on a garden railway in northern California's Zone 9. Rich Abate loves to scratchbuild truly scale structures from the town and era in which he and his brother grew up. Ed Abate loves to garden and they both run trains in their Rooster Creek Railroad. Lending scale to the magnificent hotel and a colorful little park are two dwarf Alberta spruce trees, clipped to represent healthy street trees. For a pruning lesson, follow steps in Chapter 8, "Prune trees for a scale appearance."

Were it not for the crossing signals at Adobe Mountain Railroad Park, you might think you had stumbled into a ghost town in the Wild West, here in Arizona's Zone 10. The Arizona Garden Railway Society keeps the native shrubbery trimmed near the buildings of their 7.5"-gauge ride-on railway, which borrows scenery from the surrounding hills. To create a grassy scene in your scale of choice, read Chapter 16, "Grass-like miniatures."

If it didn't rain every afternoon, Nancy and Werner Leupold would have to water their garden every day. The air is moist but the soil is non-existent. Any added amendment sifts down through the volcanic lava rock in short course on this part of the big island of Hawaii, Zone 11. Native ferns look like tropical trees and spread underground by runners, popping up wherever they can. They are both boon and doom, because they have to be pulled from the track on their Leupold Garten Bahn. Good ol' juniper and shrubby lemon-lime thyme, both poor-soil lovers, can make it with a little TLC. The unusual succulent "tree" is *Pedilanthus* sp., related to a native of Florida, where it thrives in sandy soil. For plants that easily survive with little moisture, see Chapter 12, "Deserts need succulents."
Werner Leupold photo

A birdbath doubles as an appropriate mini-garden container at Foster Botanical Garden in Zone 11's Honolulu, Hawaii. Matching pebbles hold down the water-loving roots of a palm-like clump of dwarf papyrus (*Cyperus papyrus* 'King Tut' or *C.p.* 'Nanus', Zones 9-11, grown as an annual in cooler zones). Public gardens are great resources for finding climate-suitable plants for your garden. In the Appendix, map out "Miniature gardens you can visit," then go!

1

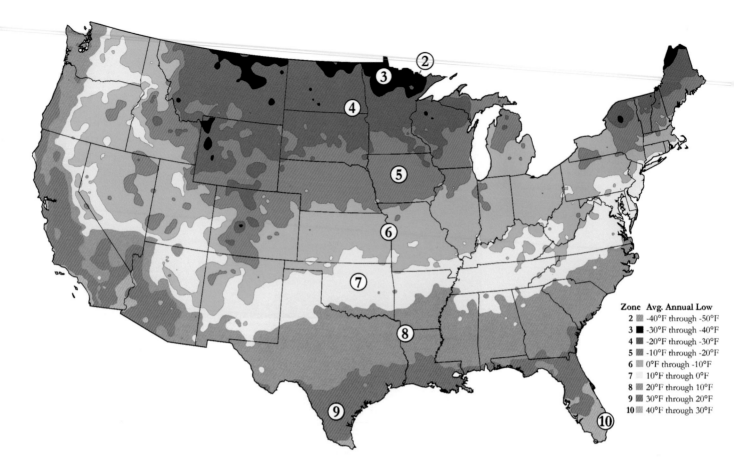

Hardiness zone maps
by www.arborday.org
Used with permission

Zone	Avg. Annual Low
2	-40°F through -50°F
3	-30°F through -40°F
4	-20°F through -30°F
5	-10°F through -20°F
6	0°F through -10°F
7	10°F through 0°F
8	20°F through 10°F
9	30°F through 20°F
10	40°F through 30°F

2

'Zoning laws' for climate compatibility

Hardiness Zones are the answer to the question, "Where can I grow this plant?" If you're planting strictly native plants, you won't need to worry. Your nursery plants were originally plucked from all over the world and then researchers tried to grow them in every imaginable climate. The US Department of Agriculture (USDA) compiled a list of hardiness ratings measured by the lowest temperature at which each plant will survive with normal cultivation practices. The USDA Hardiness Zones are the standard used in this book and most resources.

Read the tag

Most reputable nurseries now include an information tag on both herbaceous and woody perennials so that gardeners have a better chance of finding plants that will make it through the winter months as well as the heat of summer. The standard has always been (in the USA as well as some other countries) the USDA Hardiness Zones, from 1 to 11. Zone 1 has the coldest winter in interior Alaska and Zone 11 has the warmest winter in Hawaii's coastal areas. Zones 2 through 10 have also been subdivided into "a" and "b" zones, so that, for example, Zone 5a has a colder average low temperature than Zone 5b. In this book, as on most plant tags, we will stick to whole numbers. The temperature ranges are averages, not assurances of minimum temperature.

These zones refer to perennials only. Annuals are expected to live only one season and are chiefly used to add color during the summer until the first killing frost, although their seeds may sprout in spring. Herbaceous perennials die to the ground in winter and their roots live on. Woody perennials are shrubs and trees.

Gardeners need to learn which hardiness zone they live in because local garden centers will play tricks on customers and offer deliciously enticing exotic perennials. Of course you want them to survive the winter, but sadly, they just don't have it in their DNA. The honest nurseries will post a sign as I saw recently in Calgary, Alberta, "Dwarf Alberta spruce is not cold hardy here." Savvy gardeners are willing to risk growing these plants and baby them during the coldest temperatures with mulches, burlap wraps or windbreaks of wooden tents.

Climate change

In 2006 the Arbor Day Foundation updated the USDA Hardiness Zones map to show the climate change since 1990. Although the plants still have the same zone rating, your town may have less severe winters and warmer summers. The maps here will show you how your area is rated for cold hardiness. If you are unsure of how to read the map or if you think you're on the edge of a zone, plug in your ZIP code at www.

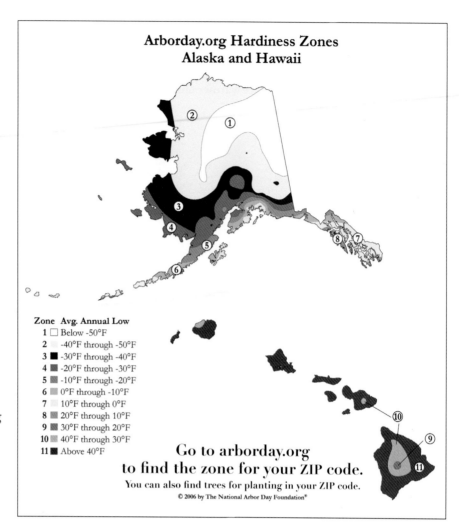

Arborday.org Hardiness Zones
Alaska and Hawaii

Zone	Avg. Annual Low
1	Below -50°F
2	-40°F through -50°F
3	-30°F through -40°F
4	-20°F through -30°F
5	-10°F through -20°F
6	0°F through -10°F
7	10°F through 0°F
8	20°F through 10°F
9	30°F through 20°F
10	40°F through 30°F
11	Above 40°F

Go to arborday.org
to find the zone for your ZIP code.
You can also find trees for planting in your ZIP code.

arborday.org/webtools/hortzones/ziplookup.cfm?RegID=1014.

Once you know your zone, say Zone 5, and buy a plant labeled Zones 5-8, you might want to note that you're growing it at the lowest recommended temperatures. If you live in one of the warmest zones of 9-11 and buy a plant rated for Zones 3-8, the plant may not get enough winter dormancy (rest) or survive the summer heat.

Live in Great Britain?

- Here's the link for Great Britain's Hardiness Zones: http://www.trebrown.com/hrdzone.html
- Europe's map and zones are here: http://www.uk.gardenweb.com/forums/zones/hze.html
- Australia's map and zones are here: http://www.anbg.gov.au/gardens/research/hort.research/zones.html.

Actually, you can type "Any country" plus "Hardiness Zone" into an online search engine for its map and zones. Canadian and European nurseries use

the USDA Hardiness Zone criteria for ornamental plants including miniatures.

How hot?

In addition to Cold Hardiness Zones, some plant tags (Monrovia Nursery, for example) come with Heat Tolerance Zones. The scale allows you to gauge whether to try a plant in your area.

For instance, I chose a Shaina Japanese maple, which is rated OK for Heat Tolerance Zones 2-8, but I chanced it in Zone 9. I was betting that the afternoon shade and spray from a water feature would help it thrive. Five years later, it's fine and strong, but it does look a bit sun-dried during a rare 100-degree heat spell, which burns leaf margins (edges) brown from desiccation. Read how to prevent this in Chapter 7, "Mini-plant care."

Plants rest at night, and it's actually the hot night temperatures that exhaust the Zone 3-8 plant in Zone 9. Gardens on the coast with cool night temperatures have better luck.

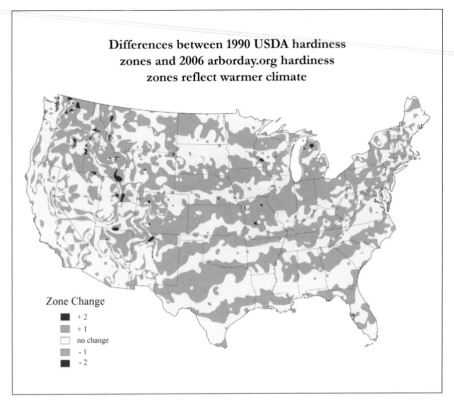

Differences between 1990 USDA hardiness zones and 2006 arborday.org hardiness zones reflect warmer climate

Zone Change
- ■ + 2
- ▨ + 1
- □ no change
- ▨ - 1
- ■ - 2

If you fall in love with a Zone 2-8 Shaina Japanese maple (left), you'll tolerate the leaf tips getting a bit browned in your Zone 9 garden in order to enjoy this kind of color all season. On the right, three Nana Emperor dwarf pomegranates (Zones 7-10) were appropriately planted in the Ditmers' O&OE.

Microclimates

Within your hardiness zone and within your yard, microclimates lurk, ready to take your young ones. Inexplicably, plants, which are supposedly correct for your area, will wilt and die or never emerge from the ground in spring. Valleys, hills, bodies of water, wind, moisture, soil, neighboring plants, pets, and the mass of buildings are some of the conditions affecting climate in your garden. You just have to learn about your area. The nursery down the street, local garden clubs, and online blogs will tell their sad stories about what happens when nature gets the best of the garden.

Sunset Publishing Co. has done a great job of explaining microclimates created by hills and bodies of water on the US west coast. Sunset created a new rating system for that area, numbered Sunset Zones 1-24, which are referred to in Sunset books. These numbers are not used on plant tags, however, and we will not use them in this book, which has a global readership.

In the last photo, microclimates in this yard include high-and-dry slopes, sun-baked stacked rocks, deep cool shade, high-traffic hardpan, low boggy spots, wet pools, and maybe even urine-soaked soil near dog runs.

In Part 3, "Plant Selection," instruction and charts will tell you which plants might fill the needs of those problem areas within your hardiness zone. If you're looking for a cozy place to winter over a tender perennial, plant it near your house, where the climate is several degrees warmer due to residual heat loss.

Planting season

Springtime seems to awaken the gardener in all of us and then by fall, we're busy battening down the hatches for winter. Your plants are getting ready for winter, too. Cold temperatures initiate dormancy and the tops stop growing, but some plants continue to grow underground until full dormancy, when metabolism has all but stopped.

One last suggestion for increased winter-survival is to transplant new plants in the fall or late summer. Giving new plants cooler nights but warm days allows them to get a good start setting down roots. Be sure to distress the root ball (Chapter 7). After looking at great gardens all summer you should have collected a nice list of plants to buy. Nurseries often have sales in the fall and you'll get a larger size plant than in springtime—it's a good deal for plants and your purse.

Microclimates within your garden mirror the same temperature fluctuations found in full-scale towns. Cold settles in low areas, drying wind speeds up on hills, shade creates damp cold conditions, and sun dries out some plants. Buildings hold heat and release warmth to help nearby plants in winter, but walls can also reflect too much of the sun's heat in summer. Moving tender, fussy plants often helps them find the right home. The cut-leaf foliage on this Trost's dwarf birch (*Betula pendula* 'Trost's Dwarf', Zones 3-9) enjoys the increased humidity near the stream and portrays the classic weeping willow, another water lover in the Ogdens' PCRR.

2

Design your mini garden

3

Design is part structure, part ingredients, and part personal flair. Some gardeners appear to have a natural sense of design, planting one petite plant after another until everything looks gorgeous, seemingly without any instruction manual. In reality every yard comes with a recipe, and in this chapter and those that follow, you'll find the ingredients for a luscious garden of miniature plants for all seasons. You just need to spice it up with your own creative juices.

Fantasy and reality—this little park emerged from the author's imagination, but it could be a park in Anytown, USA. Irish moss (*Sagina subulata*, Zones 5-10) blossoms are practically microscopic on the lawn. English ivy (*Hedera helix* 'Jeanette', Zones 6-10) climbs the gazebo. Three cutleaf birch park trees (*Betula pendula* 'Trost's Dwarf', Zones 3-9) provide light shade and mimic weeping willow trees in phase 1 of Don and Marilyn Pickett's "Pickett Line."

This strong theme, Dart and Dot Rinefort's mining operation, repeats the wooden trestles, rustic buildings, lots of dwarf red cedars and a couple of different groundcovers. All details support the rural scene.

Jerry and Alison Ogden replaced their lawn with a theme park, modeling Uintah Railway. Viewing from three sides allows for a virtual ride on the model trains. In summer, an umbrella shaped coral-bark Japanese maple shades visitors from their vantage facing the south. *Jerry Ogden photo*

Time and budget constraints will help you determine the overall scope, but if you start with a small area or "phase 1", then you'll learn as you go. Happily, it's the personalized innovations that are innocently discovered while exploring, which make each garden uniquely interesting. In a sophisticated age when we can visit manicured mini gardens at Disney and other parks, some novice gardeners are afraid to venture into miniature gardening or modeling railways outdoors. Maybe we don't have a Disney budget, but we all have a small place to decorate with miniature plants to create a big scene.

The difference between a full-scale landscape and a miniature garden

The corky winged bark of the deciduous dwarf burning bush (*Euonymus alatus* 'Compacta', Zones 4-8) gets noticed in the front of the layout during winter. In the fall, somewhat large leaves blaze in magenta red, creating the depth perception that trees behind it are farther away. It's a view block which somewhat hides the portal.

is your footprint. Whereas we are intended to walk in and around your backyard as in a park, the miniature landscape is usually meant for viewing only. A well-composed miniature landscape greets your eyes with captivating charm, guides your attention to points of interest, invites you to linger at various scenes until their story is told, then sends you off in search of new sites to explore. Curiosity, amazement, and the feeling of being small enough to travel the rails and verdant paths keep us transfixed when the mini garden is working well.

Where do we start? Rather than just digging holes for pretty little plants, you will find your green thumb turning blue from blueprints. Be your own civil engineer and plot out how to pull the whole layout together and still allow for rights of way and infrastructure. After all is done, you will need to maintain it, preferably with enjoyment, so starting with that awareness will determine much of your garden's structure. Before breaking ground, let's look at some design principles, which differ only slightly from full-scale landscaping.

Theme and scheme

In a tiny fantasyland or replica of a geographical place, the living elements, like the trees and groundcover, paint the picture in three-dimensional, ever-changing authenticity. Choose the setting for your story by visualizing a

geographical landscape you've visited on trips around the globe or within your imagination. If reality is the goal, study photos to replicate a place. Rail fans like to model their favorite railroad, often replicating a historical period. Or would you like to wing it and create a fantasy?

Then there's pure whimsy! Unexplainable urges to include an obviously out-of-scale element lighten the serious task of finding the meaning of life. Go ahead and make us smile. The fun of using miniature plants is only bound by your imagination, available time and space, and nature's order. I hesitate to create too much structure in the theme department, but if it's scale accuracy you're after, this book will help.

Here are examples of geography, modeled accurately, but in various styles. Northern boreal forests ultimately grow pointy fir and spruce trees, portrayed by dwarf conifers. Nearby areas, which appear to be recovering from deforestation, can be represented by swaths of deciduous broadleaf shrubs. Or you can choose to plant the whole forest with tiny little trees, each meticulously clipped to bonsai beauty. Another gardener will plant sprawling, mounding shrubs behind a few little trees to represent the continuation of the forest in the distance. All get the scene painted but the latter is the least time consuming.

As a master gardener, Alison's number one request was to have the garden railway be integrated into the yard, which was aided by repetition of plants from the full-scale yard into the railway. Of seasonal winter interest, their bright red, full-sized coral bark Japanese maple (*Acer palmatum* 'Sango Kaku', Zones 4-9) is mirrored in miniature to its right. Both contrast with the pink spring plum blossoms. *Jerry Ogden photo*

Depth perception of scale

Creating the illusion that some objects are much farther away is the most desired design concept by modelers in mini gardens. In a small landscape, it's critical to notice the shape of leaves and profile of plants, as in the example of the northern forest above, to keep gardening fun and not drudgery. Only a few rules apply if depth of field is your goal. Larger (not crazy big) leaves, if placed in the foreground, force your comparison of the smaller leaves just beyond to seem much smaller. Occasionally a taller open-branched tree in the foreground will cause you to peer through the limbs as if you were perched there viewing the scene. See Chapter 8 "Prune trees for a scale appearance."

It seems backward at first to obstruct part of your hard work, but planting an occasional view block in front is a ploy to urge us to physically move on in the garden. Where's the train going? What's beyond that point? Keep us somewhat unquenched.

Focal-point scenes play out in the central, often largest area of the layout where little-leafed plants complement objects, like buildings and trains.

Position rocks or small-leafed hills of shrubs way in the rear to create the backdrop. A garden in scale feels in harmony.

Two more optical aids to depth perception are height and color. Height is obvious—within a group, plant taller trees in front, shorter trees in the rear. Color is less obvious until you notice that red objects seem to jump out and grab your attention, while objects colored from the blue end of the spectrum seem distant.

If scale was your sole purpose, a red cut-leaf Japanese maple planted in the front of the garden countered by a rear hill of sprawling purplish-blue junipers wearing tiny needles would set off your middle ground scene to perfection. A white focal point in that scene will make it pop! What about shiny vs. dull—can you guess? For more on the language of color, see Chapter 5 "Color me content."

Finally, raise your railroad as close to eye level as is practical for your space and budget or everything will be far away, from your feet to the fence. See Chapter 11 "Cascading trees and the rocks that support them" for retaining wall instructions. Chapter 6 "Easy ac-

cess into your garden" shows options for building height into your layout.

Repetition vs. variety

When all items in a garden have equal value, they shout, "We're all important!" and then nothing gets top billing and the whole thing falls apart in chaos. Without repetition the principle of variety is lost in confusion, like a glass cabinet packed with treasures. One tidy way to cohesively tie your garden together is to edge the railroad or build a retaining wall with the same rock as the mountains, and then contrast that rock with a shale cliff. Keep the variety of plants to a minimum in a small garden. In larger gardens more complex combinations of color, form and texture have the space to surprise us and then later get integrated down the way by the repetition of some of those elements.

Repeat tree groups in uneven numbers, then balance the group with a contrasting specimen for variety. This concept is carried to another dimension when plants or items are massed, discussed in the next Chapter "Massing plants to frame a focal point." Taken to extremes, repetition backfires and seems disorderly or monotonous.

Japanese gardens are known for making music simply with one color, green, which they jazz up in form, texture and placement.

Mix up the height of plants to prevent them from competing with one other and keep your eyes moving over the landscape. Create a berm or little mountain for a similar effect. In a smaller garden, plant the tallest plants or mountain near the middle, preferably a third of the way from the left or right, although a symmetrical arrangement works, too – it's just more formal. If you must position a mountain far left or right, balance it with a long, low focal point on the opposite side to add weight and stability.

Group similar items in an irregular triangle, whether plants or figures, to prevent like elements from competing with each other. If two are used, place them visually on a diagonal, which is less static, more dynamic, and keeps our eyes moving.

Emphasis vs. balance

A garden can have one main focal point or several spaced over the layout. A gurgling water feature draws attention because of movement and sound. The supporting aquatic plants look natural in the water setting and soften the rock structure creating the waterfall. The relationship between the focal point and the supporting elements says, "Look at us, we're a unit." A figure or group of figures, like a herd of deer in a clearing, creates virtual action, also a focal point. Space each figure at unequal distances.

When structures or a series of structures like buildings and bridges present themselves in a landscape, they can seem foreign and call attention to their geometrical angles. They are the focal points and deserve to be complemented and helped into the landscape, usually by the plants, although gravel and rocks can do that, too.

This design principle is usually the easiest for modelers to understand because we can see that the farm needs a field and orchard, the town needs a row of street trees, and the bridge would be improved by some little grassy weeds underneath to simulate the countryside. Organic nature balances the awkwardness of angles and plumb lines.

Disney's demonstration of depth perception

To illustrate this concept, Walt Disney hosted a documentary on the making of an animated scene with Bambi, the fawn, walking in deep woods. Disney introduced an artist who painted three long transparent panels, like see-through glass landscapes layered one behind the other. Imagine first, a bottom static layer washed in dark greens with vertical fuzzy lines to show trees far off. Next, the artist pulls, right to left, a second slow-moving panel painted with thicker, densely populated trees, but we can still see the background through them. The fastest moving and closest (mostly clear) panel is sparsely colored with detailed ferns at hoof level and rough-barked trunks spaced far apart, so that as it is pulled right to left, we can see the depth of the forest. The action of Bambi and his pals takes place in front of the middle ground, which heightens the 3-D magic. The tactile proximity of the foreground moving faster than the middle ground, strengthens the sensation of "being there" because an occasional tree trunk blocks our view for an instant to refresh the scene.

Four elements in this full-scale scene illustrate how to pull off the principle of depth of field, here in Banff, Alberta, in the Canadian Rocky Mountains. First is the foreground of crusty, tactile, speckled rock, which literally supports and contrasts the second element, the focal point of the incredibly old leaning tree. Look through its shelf-like limbs to see the third part, the middle background of pointy green cones, where only the first two or three "rows" show soil around them. Finally, the hazy non-detail of the gray-blue distant trees brings our focus back to the fascinating, almost human tree, reaching out to touch us. Oh wait, now the foreground rock, repeating the same color, points to the far-off road between the lower "shelves" of the branches. A good story is circular.

To further eliminate the man-made look of full-scale structures on the horizon, use climbing vines, leaning flagstone, and shrubby trees to hide the vertical/horizontal lines of fences, decks, and sheds. Help us to stay immersed in the parallel reality.

Vantage points

One key element to keep in mind is the audience and their viewing platform. A miniature garden is as much theater as avocation. Your garden continues to play out the scenes while you're resting, and new performances should be available from various viewpoints. Create

The author used depth of field in the 7'-deep garden pictured, here viewed from the right side. On the left and middle ground area a few conifer trees were planted. On the far right of the photo, in a 3' space between the conifers and the fence, she planted three sprawling junipers (*Juniperus procumbens* nana 'Greenmound', Zones 3-9), spanning over 12' wide.

Sitting in a chair in front of Jay and Sallie Sanders' raised bed Cloud Mountain Railroad, we have an eye-level vantage, further helped by the terracing with rocks to create a deer-inhabited plateau graced by an ancient rosemary tree (*Rosmarinus officinalis* 'Prostratus', Zones 6-10). The pink boulders integrate the railway into the pink, stucco-walled yard.

Brian Wenn invites us in for another vantage point. The rear hedge encloses this room with a view and makes a great backdrop.

Two bold foreground plants of different heights balance the focal point of the pueblo-like rock. Stones of similar color surrounding the rock tie it all together on Scott Kennedy's East Bay Union Railroad.

a sunny spot for cloudy, cold days, and a canopied cool area to get away from blistering sun. Guests will be grateful for seating at all angles from the stage, especially opposite focal points, where they will look for all the surprises.

If your railroad is positioned along an east-west fence and you'll be looking into the south, then the garden elements may be shaded and back-lit much of the time. While this can be dramatic in some ways, it also means the sun beats down on your face. If shade trees along the fence are not an option, consider smaller ornamental trees in front of the railroad under which viewers can avoid the sun. Large market umbrellas or a frame for an inexpensive shade cloth canopy provide welcome relief in summer.

One of the best seats in the house for miniature gardens is at the bottom of a slope where we see a grandstand of stepped terraces at a glance. If your slope runs downhill from your living area, create a second patio or deck at the bottom so you're eye level with the little people in the little land. Looking up feels humble and helps to create the awe factor. See the links in the appendix for "Step up to terraces" in *Garden Railways*.

Integration

Scan your yard for clues about how the mini garden will augment the yard.

How can you use the above principles to tie the miniature garden into the full-scale garden? Look at the existing structures, especially the hardscape of walls, decks, patios, and walkways.

What materials can you duplicate to tell the story of the miniature world? Can you echo the flagstone from your walkways in stacked rock cliffs? Can you mirror the burgundy color of nearby trees with little shrubs, like Crimson Pygmy barberry, or do you want to repeat one of those burgundy trees within the layout for some shade? Can you integrate your swimming pool with a water feature in the mini world? What about a wooden trestle to reflect your wooden fence?

Just before entering the gate to Gary and Sue Robinson's garden railway, visitors pass an arrangement of five miniature trees in a natural canterra trough, a preview of the mini world to follow. Now over 10 years old, the group remains in harmony, balanced because of the triangular-height profile and repetition of green conifers contrasted with the red fruit of the broadleaf cotoneaster on the right. Sweet little grape hyacinths down front integrate the planter into the yard, matching the blue rosemary hedge, as does the planted feather-rock "mountain," which matches the trough and river rock beyond.

Backlit gardens have a mysterious, shadowy charm interjected with luminescent windows of color. But, a shadeless vantage point would mean viewing the garden with the sun in your eyes. Left to right, the blooms of spotted deadnettle (*Lamium maculatum* 'White Nancy', Zones 3-10), thymeleaf fuchsia (*Fuchsia thymifolia*, Zones 8-11) and dwarf thrift (*Armeria caespitosa*, Zones 4-9) catch the sun, which radiates their colors.

Look at the grade and existing trees for clues to tell you where to place mountains, plains, shaded areas and hot sunny desert lands. Many of these features will be apparent because the desert plants can't be grown in shade, a mountain needs lateral space to create height, and towns need a few flat places to "build" houses. Ponds need a low place in the sun where they won't readily fill up with leaves under trees.

Integration also means designing ways to get in and out of all areas of the layout. Be sure your path behind the layout is wide enough for you. With no access path, be sure to leave breathing room for fences so they don't rot from materials holding moisture. Although you might not need steps up the slope now, might you in 10 years? For more ideas see Chapter 6, "Easy access into your garden."

Pencil and paper and plans

First, assess your available space. On a piece of paper, preferably graph paper, plot the perimeter of your prospective landscape, then plot where all the full-scale structures in the yard will remain.

Fences are a good place to start. These benchmarks usually provide

Triangles are more pleasing than rows or squares in groupings. The three waterfalls form an irregular triangle of different heights and are supported by the eye-catching red roof, tea tree and red maple, which also form a triangle.

straight lines with posts that can be used for finding grid points on the ground. Numbering the posts or labeling them with a landmark on the paper will help you sort out where you are on the "map." Measure distances perpendicular to the posts and plot as much information as is pertinent on the paper. If there is a slope, indicate that with arrows. Label the slope with an arrow pointing uphill or with elevation rings as on topographical maps. Show the outline of a tree canopy, if it will make shade a limiting factor. Keep it simple.

Sketch the outline of any hardscape features you intend to incorporate into the landscape, like retaining walls, water features, and paths. Plan for underground electrical or plumbing conduit. The track diagram is also part of the hardscape and acts like a border to planting beds, which portray the countryside. Once the railroad, retaining walls and paths are plotted on paper, you will find a relatively small area to landscape with plants, depending on how elaborate your infrastructure is.

Now use design principles to place groups of plants within planting areas. Some plants will decorate little buildings. Go to Chapters 9-19 in Part 3, "Plant Selection," make a mini-plants list for working with your plan. Later, when you've built the hardscape, feel free to shift potted plants around on the ground for optimal effect before planting begins. For help on planting, go to Chapter 7, "Mini-plant care." Ideally, come back to this chapter after reading the entire book.

Exploration

Studying photos is good, visiting layouts is better, but "doing" is best. Few railroad gardeners who have seen some photos, read some magazines, and then jumped in building their own layout won't deny that they learned volumes on their first attempt. Many will also agree that they changed their layout once they saw how others built theirs, because they knew what wasn't working and could see a way to improve it.

It's comparatively easy to change a few things in a miniature garden. See the Appendix for gardens to visit, clubs to join, online links, and publications.

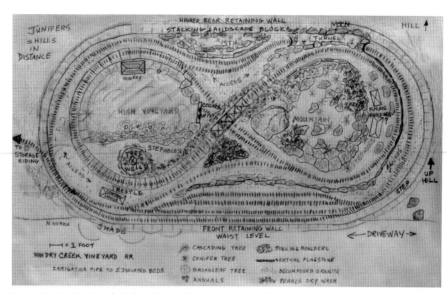

Dave Stare's Dry Creek Railroad provides a good example of a plan designed for someone who wanted a low-maintenance garden, but lots of opportunities for operating trains. Note that planted areas are isolated by gravel, which carries the theme of the dry creek through the middle of the layout…

…with a simple design with lots of access…

…paints a picture of happiness.

4

Mass planting to frame a focal point

1. The frame and matting gently guide our view inward and cause our eyes to pause to assimilate the story within. Likewise, the meadow of inch-tall star creeper (*Pratia pedunculata* 'County Park', Zone 5-9) gives us an uninterrupted view, funneling us into the farmyard. The split-rail fence and five, lined-up apple trees (*Cotoneaster microphyllus* 'Emerald Spray', Zone 5-8) help frame the yard where Bubba is tending the horses.

The design principle of massed plantings in home landscaping is a relatively new concept but textural, green drifts and colorful swaths are now standard practice along highways to mimic the countryside growth along roads. Simply put, massing is a group of like elements—more than three or four. Massing is impressive because of sheer numbers or weight, like a long freight train that makes us stop to count the cars or marvel at the pulling power of the engine. Then, curiosity draws us in to notice the components—in this case, the cars.

Continuity

Grouping elements, like groundcover, trees, rocks, or structures, serves several purposes in railway design. Aesthetically, masses can frame focal points (photos 1 and 2), separate themes, or provide visual balance. Physically, massing groundcover or stones allows access into the garden. For practicality, covering the ground reduces maintenance by inhibiting weeds. Psychologically, the most compelling reason for bulk plantings is that their bold, dramatic statements create a sense of order and an awareness of space. Many an amateur has discovered the difficulty in merging a wide range of dissimilar plants into a pleasing palette for comfortable viewing over a long period of time. "Keep it simple" is the rule of the day.

Preventing a hodgepodge and limiting the type of plants used is hard for us horticulturists. I want to experience them all, so I've created a little nursery of potted, railway wannabes. Now I watch my "hopefuls" for clues as to how to landscape them in. Some will be specimens (focal points) in stand-alone places of importance.

Replication

Another technique for pulling the railway together is repetition of the same species or type of plant in various locations. In photo 2, we grouped similar, needle-leaf evergreens in a forest. While we appreciate their differences, they do lose some of their uniqueness in exchange for acting as a unit. The slight differences and sizes make the forest more believable. A meadow of several same-size groundcovers has a similar naturalizing effect. The nice thing is you won't have to try to get this effect, as weeds and other groundcover seeds blow in—just like in the wild.

Repeating a color shows you where to look, as your eyes naturally bounce from one color to a similar hue. The house and rocks in photo 1 match the wooden frame to bind the look harmoniously. In photo 3, the stacked rocks match the color of the boulders, thus carrying the color to create a more dramatic mass of a cliff. Yes, there is variation but the rust tells the story of minerals exposed when the railroad company cut away the mountain. In photo 4, orange is bounced between the engine and the standard tree rose; and the 11 micro-miniature, light-pink roses (*Rosa* sp.

2. Stepping back 12 feet from Bubba's ranch on Don and Marilyn Pickett's Danville, Alamo & Little Creek Railroad, the bigger picture shows the actual frame—a mass of evergreen trees, mostly dwarf Alberta spruce (*Picea glauca* 'Conica', Zone 3-8) and dwarf false cypress (*Chamaecyparis thyoides* 'Little Jamie', Zone 3-8). These tall trees frame the ranch by hiding the neighbor's fence beyond and separating the ranch from other scenes. The bushy tree at right is a flowering "specimen" (*Fuchsia thymifolia*, Zone 8-11).

3. In Ken and Pat Martin's Somerset-Pacific Railroad, massed gray rocks of two types— bouquet-canyon flagstone and natural, volcanic, feather-rock boulders—create a steep retaining wall. Ken is modeling Pardee Point, a famous cutaway on the East Tennessee & Western North Carolina Railroad.

Ask the masters

Zones listed are USDA Hardiness Zones

Question: How has the design concept of "massing" helped you tell the story of your railway?

Scott Osterweil
Near Boston Massachusetts, Zone 6
I use small-scale plants around key scenes on my railroad to maintain visual interest [in the focal points], but I also use larger plants that create "view blocks" and isolate those scenes. For those blocks I particularly like vertical forms.

Ray Turner
San Jose, California, Zone 9
Here, I created the deep canyon inspired by the High Line on the Durango & Silverton. I also wanted a high deck-truss for its visual appeal. The massive rockwork (cast concrete) creating the canyon contributes to the ruggedness of the scene. At the same time, it provides visual separation between two town areas, Mystic and North End. Mystic, just to the left of the truss bridge, is the high point of the railroad and the entrance to the helix. The passenger train disappearing into the canyon will soon arrive at North End, which has the yard and engine servicing facilities for the Mountain Division.

Bob and Sharon "Sky" Yankee
Mulino, Oregon, Zone 7
Yes, we do a lot of massing to set a scene. However, in setting all that up, some looking ahead is a good idea. Since we mostly use trees, we have to calculate how much time it will take for them to grow together and then how far apart they should be planted. Most reference guides will list how much a tree will grow in a year. For instance the dwarf Alberta spruce (*Picea glauca* 'Conica', Zone 3-8) is listed as 3-6" a year. The 6" is under perfect growing conditions and probably with a lot of fertilizer, which we don't recommend. The 3" represents when the Alberta has to struggle more. Its sport, the Jean's Dilly is listed as growing ½ to 3" a year. We have never seen it grow much more than ½", even in near-perfect Pacific Northwest conditions. Therefore, we can plant the Jean's Dilly trees closer together than the faster-growing Alberta spruce. In massing trees, we plant at irregular intervals to replicate nature and quite often leave an opening for the unexpected view, such as the distant vista of the Fire Tower at Angel's Camp. Even with the best planning we found that 10 years later our Little Jamie trees have filled out more than expected and now have to be trimmed to keep the view open.

A massing of evergreen trees behind the town separates the town from the untamed country. *Cecil Easterday photo*

Cecil Easterday
Near Columbus, Ohio, Zone 5
The Sparta & Shelby Railroad is very large, so the suggestions here might not be practical for smaller railroads. In the small farming town of Sparta, houses are far apart, with large yards and lots of trees. They are separated from the town by fields and trees. To recreate that feel in the garden railroad, a town was developed first, with buildings representing all of the services you would typically find in a small town (including a movie house). Several yards away, the residential area was set with homes spread far apart with separate landscaping. I wanted the railroad to look good in winter as well as summer, so most of the plants look the same in winter or have winter interest.

The forest includes several varieties of dwarf spruce (all Zone 3-8): *Picea glauca* 'Jean's Dilly'; *Picea glauca conica* (dwarf Alberta); *Picea abies* 'Nidiformis' (birdsnest dwarf Norway); and *Picea abies* 'Pumila'. For a variety of textures, there are several broadleaf evergreens, like boxwood, (*Buxus* 'Green Velvet', Zone 5-8) and dwarf barberry for red color (*Berberis thunbergii* 'Bagatelle', Zone 4-8). Getting closer to the "residential" section of town, we used lighter and lower plants: *Chamaecyparis pisifera* 'Tsukumo' (Zone 3-8); *Juniperus horizontalis* 'Mother Lode' (yellow-green foliage, Zone 3-9); *Juniperus procumbens* 'Nana' (needs to be trimmed to keep the size under control, Zone 4-9); *Picea abies* 'Echiniformis' (blue-gray, Zone 3-8); and *Juniperus squamata* 'Blue Star' (Zone 4-8).

For the lawns, it depends on whether a uniform lawn is needed or a "scruffy

This fire-tower scene, surrounded by dwarf Alberta spruce trees, is on Ray Turner's line but well illustrates Sky's scene on her railway. *Ray Turner photo*

4

The sheer size of this gorge calls attention to the scene but also divides adjacent scenes to allow them to have their own story. To see and hear this scene go to *www.youtube. com/watch?v=cR9Kna50Y20.*
Ray Turner photo

lawn" is the thing. My favorite for a low and tight-growing lawn is *Lysimachia japonica* 'Minutissima' (miniature moneywort, Zone 4-8). For less formal yards, I have used *Ophiopogon japonicus* 'Nippon' (mondo grass, Zone 6-11); *Acaena microphylla* (a very aggressive grower, Zone 6-8); *Ajuga reptans* 'Chocolate Chip' (Zone 4-9); *Sedum hispanicum* (Zone 5-9); *Leptinella (Cotula) squalida* 'Platt's Black' (dark, almost black, Zone 5-11); and *Leptinella (Cotula) minor* (green, Zone 3-11).

Mass planting groundcover on a square grid leaves gaps as the plants fill in.

Starts planted in a triangular pattern appear fuller and more natural as plants grow together.

Figure 1
Stagger plants rather than aligning them in perfect rows. The look is more organic, and the occasional lost plant won't be so obvious.

4. On the DA&LCRR, three complementary, miniature-rose varieties are grouped together *en masse*, almost knocking us over with the impact of their floriferous performance. Even the rosy sedum next to the track (lower left) carries the theme.

5. In The Living Desert's railroad, ledger rocks create a continuous terrace above pink succulents, tying the scenes together. Trees are massed in the distance to block the scene beyond. Silver carpet (*Dymondia margaretae*, Zone 9-11) carpets a room and unifies this section.

6. Neil Ramsay's Emerald Isle from the June 2009 *Garden Railways* cover feature. Mass planting of *Lonicera nitida* provides a unified look to the whole railway. *Marc Horovitz photo*

'Baby Austin', Zone 5-10) are grouped in drifts, then repeated, to expand the scene and frame the quartzite-rock outcropping, the focal point.

Proximity
In "Ask the masters," opposite page, Sky theorizes on the relativity of spacing trees, so let's look at planting groundcover here. On the plant tag is a recommended spacing, which is often 6-10", meaning from center to center of each small plant. To avoid wasteful crowding or lingering bare spots, it's best to space the individual plants in staggered rows (triangular

pattern), rather than lined up like soldiers (square grid), as shown in figure 1.

Unity
No single garden railway that I've seen has epitomized massed planting's benefits as much as Neil Ramsay's line, the June 2009 cover story. Neil's panorama of Ireland's sweeping, rolling hills was simply done to frame his Irish trains and take us on a virtual excursion of the emerald isle. Using a limited number of plants creates a quiet, classy look, affording a sense of retreat from business, with time and space to do what we like … run trains.

5

Color me content

1. All built from recycled materials, this color-coordinated area of the Golden Gate Express Garden Railway models (left to right) Coit Tower, Ghirardelli Square, California Academy of Science's rooftop garden, the Japanese Tea Garden's pagoda, Golden Gate Bridge, and the glass-walled Conservatory of Flowers.

I recently took a turn manning our club's amazing garden railway at San Francisco's Conservatory of Flowers. Unsuspecting visitors dropped their jaws at first sight of the miniature trees and flowers among the traveling trains. The small-world, indoor version of the conservatory shines in Golden Gate Park's monochromatic (all one hue) red and white garden. Intense red azaleas, poinsettias, and cyclamens are contrasted by the diffuse silver/blue foliage of santolinas, cedars, cyclamens, and lamiums (photo 1).

2. The dominant, saturated, blue and orange buildings attract each other and us. Adjacent similar colors integrate the items, drawing us into the town's story. Note the blue star creeper *(Pratia pedunculata*, 'County Park', Zone 5-10) between the tracks and behind the café. Detail-oriented Rich and Ed Abate use the Coca-Cola sign to repeat the saloon's color, visually tying it all together on their Rooster Creek Railway.

3. A scheme of bright secondary colors, purple verbena (*Verbena* 'Tapien Blue Violet', Zone 8-11) and the orange flowers of dwarf pomegranate (*Punica granatum* 'Nana Emperor', Zone 7-11), is somewhat softened by the bushy yellow breath of heaven (*Coleonema pulchellum* 'Sunset Gold', Zone 9-11) on the left and the chartreuse mountain groundcover, Scotch moss (*Sagina subulata* 'Aurea', Zone 4-9). Even the neutral wood of the fence, bridge, and similar rock color blend in harmony around Mike and Holly Crane's Crooked Creek.

Ask the masters

Zones listed are USDA Hardiness Zones

Question: How do you color your garden?

Sue Piper
San Diego, California, Zone 10
We tend to be pretty conservative in the selection of colors on our buildings to keep our railroad as realistic in appearance as possible. Even though our selection of colorful plants is limited by exclusively growing dwarfs and miniatures, we've found a few that brighten things right up. We enjoy the tiny, beautiful splashes of lavender provided by our rosemary tree (*Rosmarinus officinalis*, Zone 9-10) and the hot-pink or white

blossoms of New Zealand tea trees (*Leptospermum scoparium*, Zone 9-11), which all bloom several times each year. The very bright-red "apples" of our thyme-leaf and gray cotoneasters (*Cotoneaster microphyllus* var. *thymifolius*, Zone 5-9) remain on the trees most of the year and are always a big hit with visitors. My favorite, considering white a color, is the tiny white daisies of *Bellium minutum* (Zone 5-9). These beauties let you know spring is really here and continue blooming through fall in our area. The daisies close up at night and open again when the sun comes out. You can't help but be cheered up just looking at the little guys!

Dick Friedman
Sacramento, California, Zone 9
Colorful flowers on trees and shrubs would be microscopic at even 1:20.3 scale, let alone the 1:32 scale I try to model! Having said that, let me also say that everything in my garden is not shades of green! I have color in the form of micro-miniature roses, whose tiny blossoms are still oversized, but I like the way they look. I also grow ajugas or *Ajuga reptans*, Zone 3-9 (I hate the name "bugleweed!") and, despite its rather dark-green foliage, in the spring and summer it puts out pretty, bright-blue spikes of flowers about 6" tall. They

Lewisia blossoms (*Lewisia longipetala* x *cotoledon*, Zone 4-8) offer springtime scale color on Ray's Mystic Mountain Railroad. "Cliff maids" love good drainage at their crowns. *Ray Turner photo*

Cecil prefers subtle color with a few eye-popping spots. In spring, the azaleas, rhododendrons, and weeping Japanese maples provide that color. *Cecil Easterday photo*

Miniature daisies brighten the median between two rail lines, reminiscent of Ladybird Johnson's Highway Beautification Program of 1965, in which sunflowers and other colorful annuals and perennials were planted along roadsides. *Sue Piper photo*

Dick's daughter, Sara, made a consist of table decorations for his retirement party. *Dick Friedman photo*

Lots of green provides year-round texture and continuity in the Rocky Lights Railroad. *Kevin Ylvisaker photo*

don't look like any earth trees but they scale out to about 16' tall, so they give some height next to the track. Maybe this summer, my miniature pomegranate (*Punicum granatum* 'Nana Emperor', Zone 7-11) will bear fruit, so red ping-pong balls hanging on the tiny tree will brighten up a corner of the railway.

Ray Turner
San Jose, California, Zone 9
I have some bright-red Lewisia in the springtime. Red makes a bold statement about the end of winter and is a strong color next to the greens of spring. Red really stands out in a field of greens and browns. I also have some large fields of woolly thyme, which present a beautiful, purple carpet of springtime flowers.

Kevin Ylvisaker
Mukwonago, Wisconsin, Zone 4B
We are in Zone 4B so we get all the seasons. Spring color comes from miniature bulb stock that is planted in color groupings throughout the railway. On occasion, I will plant a few smaller annuals to give an immediate shot of color, but the focus

in the railway is green. We plant ever-greens so the railway looks great all year and any other color is a nice surprise. Evergreens are planted for both color and texture. We try to keep blue greens, like the junipers and fescue, together, and then yellow-greens, like some of the cedars and dwarf Alberta spruces, near each other. They are planted so the eye travels in and around the railway to the buildings and other plant groupings.

Cecil Easterday
Columbus, Ohio area, Zone 5
Consistent year-round color in the Sparta & Shelby Railroad is supplied by plants chosen for their foliage. Listed are some of my favorite colorful evergreens: Rheingold arborvitae (*Thuja occidentalis* 'Rheingold', Zone 2-7); Green Velvet boxwood (*Buxus* 'Green Velvet', Zone 5-9); Gold Thread false cypress (*Chamaecyparis pisifera filifera* 'Gold Thread', Zone 4-9); and Silver Queen wintercreeper (*Euonymus fortunei* 'Silver Queen', Zone 4-9) turns slightly pink in winter). Junipers come in gold, silver, and blue: *Juniperus horizontalis* 'Mother Lode'

(Zone 3-9); *J. conferta* 'Silver Mist' (Zone 6-9); *J. squamata* 'Blue Star' (Zone 4-8). Dwarf Canadian spruce (*Picea glauca* 'Rainbow's End', Zone 3-8) has mid-summer bright, creamy-yellow growth and bird's nest spruce (*Picea abies* 'Little Gem', Zone 3-8) is a true dwarf Norway spruce with tiny, light-green needles.

In summer, annuals that supply color are *Alternanthera ficoidea* 'Purple Threadleaf' (Zone 8-10), coleus, pixie impatiens, and sweet alyssum. The woody *Berberis thunbergii* 'Bagatelle' (Zone 4-8) has brick-red barberry leaves turning brighter red in the fall. My favorite grass-like plants are golden var-iegated sweet flag (*Acorus gramineus* 'Ogon', Zone 6-9) and mondo grass (*Ophiopogon planiscapus* 'Nigrescens', Zone 6-10) with purple-black foliage and pretty pink blossoms. My favorite groundcovers include stonecrops (*Sedum* sp., Zone 3-8) with foliage ranging from pink and red to several shades of green. Greek yarrow (*Achillea ageratifolia* 'Utah', Zone 4-8) is less than 1" tall spreading or cascading with gray-green foliage and bright yellow flowers.

4. Ed Assaf enjoys a medley of greens in his railway. From a sophisticated scheme of green trees and groundcover, color pops off leaves with white or yellow variegation, blue/silver waxy coatings, or yellow/red tints. Subtle differences in texture, like the rocks with the portal, extend and enrich the gray.

5. Chris and Nola Greenwald's Grunenenwald Berg Bahn incorporates masses of silvery plantings integrated into the surrounding yard. Scratchbuilt, weathered buildings add to the 1920s rural feel.

This article's title hints at the emotion and contentment that well-appointed color combinations offer but the *con*-tent of color in your railway garden also determines what we see and where our vision travels. Photo 2 proves that opposites do attract! Shops painted in polar opposites on the color wheel beckon us down the street. Next we notice the supporting, repeated shades in vehicles, signs, and little flowers. Framing the scene with tree leaves is heart-warming, healthy green. No wonder Asian culture teaches green is the frequency associated with our heart!

"Using color effectively in the garden" (*GR*, December 2003) explained the use of the color wheel in our gardens. Now let's let the color strategy of artistic gardeners inspire us to find the feeling we most want to get (and give) from our garden. For instance, photo 3 shows how "secondary" color pairings work harmoniously on a mountainside to call attention to a small water feature.

Color on (full size) buildings is a relatively new concept historically, because of the absence of affordable paint pigments and the durability of white-lead and milk-based paints. White is right if you're modeling the 1800s. For more on architectural colors, find references at *www. historichousecolors.com/books.html#general*

Is green a color?

It's in the rainbow, yet green is neutral where gardens are concerned, maybe because it's in the center of the spectrum. Without the white on this page, it would be difficult to read; without green, other colors can be jarring, when combined, and difficult to assimilate. Is green just boring? To some it is, but to others it's just perfect. Notice how unboringly the greens in photo 4 voice their cool and warm statements on either side of green, especially the Blue Star junipers (*Juniperus squamata* 'Blue Star', Zone 4-8) over the tunnel growing out of yellowish native moss. Do you feel the push-me/pull-you tactic of creating tangible tension?

The subtlety of greens and other neutral colors is why we retreat from the cities and seek out nature in the relative wilderness of parks and our backyards. Likewise, white flowers and silver leaves in the garden serve to separate awkward combinations, a kind of peace in the eye of the storm. Photo 5 could be a country roadside massed with silvery lavender cotton (*Santolina chamaecyparissus*, Zone 6-9), papery white German statice flowers (*Limonium tataricum*, Zone 4-9), and white/pink stonecrop flowers (*Sedum* sp., Zone 3-9). Gray, silver, black, brown, and white are also neutral, contributing to a naturalized look, here punctuated by yellow, button-like blooms of shrubby gray santolinas. What's natural in the southwest is blue-greens with neutral rusty browns (photo 6).

All in the timing

When I lived in the neutral-tone-saturated northeast, after eight months of dirty snow, mud, and gray, leafless trees, I wanted to plant enough vibrant color to tide

6. Not yet a rocket scientist at 10, Scott Kennedy figured out how to use color to surprise us. We're admiring the blue chalk sticks (*Senecio talinoides mandraliscae*, Zone 10-11) when a matching-colored jet suddenly crashes before our eyes into his East Bay Union Railroad.

7. Dan and Joyce Pierce go for a riot of cheerful color. The massed island of red-leaved coleus, happily shaded under the cherry tree, unifies their Train Garden within a sea of yellow marigolds and prevents cacophony.

9. Nothing subtle about this wine-colored depot shrub, volcanic wood sorrel (*Oxalis vulcanicola* 'Zinfandel', Zone 9-11 or an annual in the north) amuses passengers on the Murray's GHRR. Year-round yellow flowers close up at night.

8. Planted on a slope, an arguably out-of-scale, 6-12" high, swan-river daisy (*Brachyscome* 'Toucan Tango', Zone 9-11) spreads out to model another hillock on Richard and Melinda Murray's Green Hills Railroad. The moody blues are monochromatically blended below by the purple plains of Elfin thyme (*Thymus serpyllum* 'Elfin', Zone 4-9).

me over until the next hibernation. A good description of miniature bulbs and spring-color choices is offered in this illustrated online article: *www.donet. com/~paulrace/trains/primer/plants/spring_ color/spring_color.htm*

Other northern gardeners (see Ask the masters in this chapter) use evergreen plants, berries and beautiful bark of deciduous plants for winter color interest. Then for summer find these links in the appendix for "Colorful annuals for the railway garden" in *GR* April 2007 and the "Regional gardening reports of *GR* June 2007." In the latter issue find "Early

blooming perennials." See how one northern family colors their summer in photo 7.

Remember to shop under the shade cloth at garden centers if trees or buildings block your garden by more than a half-day of sun. Too little sun (or too few nutrients) affects color, just as too much sun can wash out color in some plants. Read labels. Now is the time to pick out a few plants for flashy fall foliage or fruit as temperatures dive.

Highlights and lowlights

One complaint I often hear regarding so-called "color" plants is that annuals and

herbaceous perennials usually sport flowers too large compared to, say, a scale figure's head. While I like to use the tiniest flowers (see sweet alyssum in Chapter 9) very close to figures and trains, I don't make it a rigid rule. How about photo 8's example: plant taller flowers in rock crevices or on a hillside to avoid height comparisons. Behind buildings, taller flowers look like bushy trees. You could save the roses, strap-leaved lilies, and larger blooms for that zone or border away from the scale objects *or* simply plant what looks and feels good to you. Over-planning has its faults. Enjoy your plants. Let them speak softly, as in photo 8, or loud and clear as in photo 9. Anyone who complains can turn off his hearing aid.

Easy access into your garden

6

1. Guests and operators ford the water via flagstones (foreground), mortared into the river's edge, to reach the shade of Don and Marilyn Pickett's central gazebo. Easy access is critical for viewing and operating the Danville, Alamo & Little Creek Railway.

Isn't it usually when guests are watching that things get stuck in inconvenient areas of the railway? When we can easily get into those remote regions, without crushing that umpteen-hour project, it's pure joy. However, one size does not fit all when it comes to solving railway access. Resourceful railroad gardeners inspired this story on innovative and inviting landscaping techniques for accessing plantings and trains.

2. In his Green Hills Railroad, Richard Murray preps his live-steam Shay to take logs to the mill. Lumber waits on the second passing siding. Both "through spurs" allow guests to get steamed up, with room for equipment underneath and on the bench to the left.

3. A train's view of an open tunnel at the Picketts' shows rebar and hardware cloth supporting cantilevered flagstone. Operators see ivy-covered rocks and clearly visible trains, which can easily be reached.

4. The Mellon Patch Railroad offers operators full view of, and easy access to, four levels of terraced track, all greened up with erosion-inhibiting groundcovers between soil-retaining boulders.

5. As Bill Mansell's backyard slopes downhill, the grade on his Left Coast Railway is kept relatively level by raising the roadbed on metal tubes at the lower end.

Pond-ering the steps

In my experience of building railways, each one unique, the muse requires time— usually days. Investigating a problem from many angles seems to tap into the cosmic bank of knowledge. While working on the obvious tasks, we keep coming back to the mystery until we gratefully see the answer staring us in the face.

Such was the case in photo 1. The civil-engineering issue was how to build a human right-of-way to a gazebo, surrounded by water, without a bulky footbridge that would obscure the waterfall. After a week of contemplating how to get safely across the water and keep it in scale, several discarded flagstones seemed to surface from nowhere. Revelation! The waterway's embankments could be flat and big enough for size 12s.

Directing traffic

Taking time to design a landscape as right as possible, before laying track, rewarded Richard and Melinda Murray with features they wouldn't have known they needed. PVC pipes, laid on the ground, represented their track layout, and daily working around these obstacles showed them where pathways and bridges were necessary.

Meanwhile, they became avid live steamers and figured out where to build a handy-but-hidden place for guests to prep steam engines at steamups (photo 2). Guests get to the rear of their railway on curving, tree lined, decomposed-granite footpaths. These paths set up like concrete (when compacted at least 6" thick), blend into the miniature scenery, and stay relatively weed free, if walked on regularly.

Walking on plants is a perfectly practical way in and out of your railway. You'll want to use "stepables," though—tough, perennial groundcovers, listed at this nursery: *www.stepables.com*. Choose from 160 non-lawn groundcovers, sorted by your USDA Hardiness Zone, then buy them locally, especially if you can find some raised near you. Be sure to note whether they require shade vs. sun exposure, and moist vs. xeric soil. The fun part is that the cool, green swath becomes the meadow or back forty for your railway structures. If guests are intended for green paths, welcome them in with occasional stepping stones.

Tunnel vision

You may remember a war movie featuring European mountains through which a

Ask the masters

Zones listed are USDA Hardiness Zones

Question: How have you provided access to your railroad or prevented the need for it?

Ray Turner
San Jose, California, Zone 9

I've learned (often the hard way) that I need to get into all areas of the railway. I was going to build a sawmill complex on the other side of the track here, but realized that I needed this space to step into the railway beyond for maintenance. So when I build it, I'm determined to make it easily removable. There is also a step built into the 18"-high rock wall, making it easy to climb into the area for work. I camouflaged the step with a stone retaining wall.

All turnouts and spurs, except the one to the mine (in the picture), are easily accessible from alongside the railway. In order to throw this turnout and uncouple cars on the mine spur, one needs to step into the railway, so I built a concrete pad next to the spur that I can step/kneel on. I covered it with ore-colored fines and debris to make it look like part of the mine-tailing piles.

Here and there on the railroad I placed a foot-sized piece of flagstone. It looks very natural (since it is natural) as part of the landscaping and gives me a place to stand or kneel to prune the plants or maintain the track.

Herb Zuegel
Near Chicago Illinois, Zone 5

Gimpyness has afflicted this geezer in his eighth decade via a bad knee. Consequently, getting the rough crud off the rails in springtime is a chore that now starts by using a plastic scrub-pad soaked with paint thinner on a broom handle instead of praying my way around the pike. Next comes more intensive running of the track-cleaning locomotive to establish good electrical conductivity on the brass rails for smooth running. Were I to start over, aluminum flex track with on-board battery power would be a better choice. As for controlling invasive

vegetation, one becomes reconciled that a surgically manipulated string-trimmer will suffice. I know of no magic re-railment remedy other than grandkids. . .if they are still low to the ground.

Sharon and Bob Yankee
Mulino, Oregon, Zone 7

Easy access is our biggest headache. Bob wanted a certain look of backwoods Oregon in the 1930s logging era. We have real dirt mountains. Some are 5-6' tall. The slopes need mountain-goat maintenance, nimble feet, and good knees, but fortunately, the dwarf and miniature trees need only occasional or no trimming. Extensive use of groundcovers and mulch, be it bark, gravel or rocks, does cut down on the weeds, which limits the use of Roundup®. However, at one open house, as I was giving a tour, a 3' thistle plant suddenly made faces at me and said, "Ha, ha, missed me!" Nope, no easy access here but lots of photo ops once the thistle was yanked out of its hiding place.

Doug Matheson
Ontario, Canada, Zone 4

While gardens and trains go well together, people traffic often does not, and a garden must be entered to be enjoyed. I use the Oriental philosophy of leading the viewer to vantage points and controlling the view and perspective. This is opposed to the Occidental idea of allowing people to go where they want, passing through a series of "garden rooms." This thinking led me to build flagstone walks and three stiles to get past elevated tracks.

Dick Friedman
Sacramento, California, Zone 9

I built my railroad in an existing garden, so I faced some of these issues back when I was installing the garden. My backyard is relatively flat, so I raised the rear of the line above the rest with concrete blocks. Now, years later, the blocks are nearly invisible in the shadows and greenery of the backyard. While building

The yard for Ray's mine, both on foundation, serves as an access step. *Ray Turner photo*

Herb's LGB track-cleaning engine gets a workout on the Elmore Elevated & Embankment line. *Herb Zuegel photo*

the railroad over the years, I've tried to leave pathways so I can get into the more remote areas to remove fallen oranges, tangerines, apples, and leaves that can obstruct the right of way!

I built my rail yard where there is a drop in elevation for a sidewalk, so I can assemble trains in the yard from a sitting position in a chair. Lastly, this past fall/winter I built a "train shed" to hold my garden-railroad stuff. I put a little door in the side of the shed so I can assemble complete trains inside and run them out, onto the railroad. I also purchased a small, rolling garden seat, which I use while working on various parts of the railroad, but sometimes I just decide to plop on the ground. Rolling all of my track-fixing tools in a couple of gondolas, I just pull them along with me as I clean joints, re-level track, and add ballast.

That's why our hobby is called "Enjoyment with everlasting challenge!"

Frank Lucas
Pleasant Hill, California, Zone 9

We designed three "hidden" paths into our railroad right at the beginning because we knew that they would be needed. But, even with these, the body still finds itself in some amazingly weird and impossible positions. (I didn't know I had muscles there!) But when I do get in there, I find that my most useful tool is the grabber in the picture. It is absolutely worth its weight in gold. Uses include lifting maple leaves out of distant bonsais; righting little people who have been knocked over by squirrels, towhees, sparrows, and cats; retrieving derailed cars from difficult locations (this usually

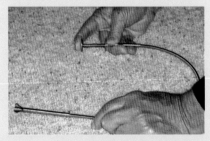

Frank won't be without his 24" Pick-up Claw, made by Great Neck, and bought at the local hardware store. *Frank Lucas photo*

happens when certifying five-year-old operators); pulling de-coupled cars out of tunnels (due to improperly modified/matched couplers); just to name a few.

Sue Piper
San Diego, California, Zone 10

In our first garden railroad, we began with a 10' x 10' area. It didn't take long to realize this wasn't big enough to do much of what we had envisioned. We did, however, learn a lot.

After much research, we decided our track should be laid on top of a trench filled with grit. We did not realize how much open area we needed for access to maintain the track or greenscaping we wanted. The only logical means of access was to walk on the track itself. Obviously, grit or other types of ballast do not provide the support required to avoid damage.

Our next attempt was based on a video purchased at a train show that demonstrated the use of 2" x 6" treated wood as a track bed. This has been a great solution for us. And, when it's been time to enlarge the railway, we just remove some screws and reuse the wood. Some of it has been in the ground for eight years with no sign of decay.

The only other advice I have is, "Bend over 'til you hurt, squat 'til it's uncomfortable, kneel for a while, and, if there's room, just sit down to recover!"

Showing the roadbed construction, 2" x 6" splices reinforce the underside of each joint. Ballast will cover the wood entirely when finished. All can be walked on. *Sue Piper photo*

train runs in a tunnel that has an open side to it (this is called a gallery), like a stone snow shed. Garden railroaders sometimes model this tunnel style on the maintenance-side of their mountains, using treated planks or concrete blocks held up by posts. We reach the trains between posts.

Photo 3 shows the author's open-tunnel project on the viewing side of a railway, where we didn't want to extend the tunnel but needed to protect the railroad from falling branches. If we had extended the 4' tunnel, we would have installed a covered irrigation box above the middle of the bore to reach stuck trains.

Tabletop operation

The less we like to crawl, the more we want to get our trains running closer to our reach. Designing retaining walls into the landscape provides easy accessibility. Yes, "planter box" railways are harder to build than ground-level lines but, once they are up, so are you! Many folks rely on local landscape companies to build walls and fill them. Then they take over building their railways, almost as if on a table in the garage. Just remember that someone (you) has to clamber onto that tabletop, so plan for stairs and buy kneepads.

Joe and Annie Mellen went a step further, where much of their railroad is the retaining wall (photo 4). Opposite, they curved their dogbone-shaped railway around a canyon for maximum reachability while standing on a dry creek bed.

"Benchwork" is another way to run trains close to waist level. Basically, the track runs on boards supported by posts (sometimes PVC pipes), often concreted into the ground. To disguise the man-made structure, shrubbery may be grown in the ground alongside or underneath, sometimes trimmed to represent trees on either side of the tracks. Hinged or lift-out bridges get you inside the loop. In the August 2002 issue of *GR*, "An innovative indoor/outdoor O-scale line" shows plans for benchwork built over a deck.

Bill Mansell recycled discarded titanium tubes from his work to build a very strong railway in the benchwork style. In photo 5, he has greened up the line by planting English-ivy vines (*Hedera helix*, Zone 4-9) on a trellis of black netting that will disappear after a few years.

6

Mini-plant care

7

As the author maintains and re-ballasts the track, she finds weeds to dig and recycle, wayward groundcover to transplant to bare spots, and dead plant material to cut out and compost. The pink false heather, lower left, needs thinning of its multiplying stems, and the dwarf conifers need opening to let in light. The water feature is becoming obscured by creeping thyme that needs trimming and the yellow flowers of the golden brass buttons in the foreground will need deadheading in a few weeks. Even though there is much to do, regular maintenance keeps the garden gorgeous.

Cultivation and maintenance of miniature garden plants require general gardening practices as well as techniques that apply specifically to diminutive plants. For example, unlike tall plants, some short plants are more likely to grow shorter distances below ground in the first few seasons, so beefing up the soil structure and root system is worth the effort for some little plants, while using poor soil is better for others. Slow-growing plants tend to be pricey, because they take a long time to grow large enough to sell, therefore it pays to learn about these little gems and garden practices in your geographical area.

Bill Allen seriously embraces the green ideology, "let no plant material leave the property." He grinds leaves for soil compost in his black "cooker." Ground-up woody branches mulch pathways.

A not-so-subtle slope of skeletons warns of the difficulty of growing plant-life (or any other life) on a steep grade.

Local growing conditions vary from county to county, let alone within the international scope of this book. The recommendation is to search locally for general information about your area. Garden centers often have a wealth of complimentary brochures and products, but you should also pick up a gardening guide or do some reading online. Family garden trains, www.btcomm.com/trains/index.htm, offers a calendar of garden tasks month by month for miniature plants. The USDA's Cooperative Extension Service in your state will have loads of information that you paid for with taxes. Their literature will specify some of your climate's issues you may encounter and how to approach them most efficiently. Ideally, look at what grows well in your area. Visit gardens.

Soil fertility

When it comes to dwarf shrubs and groundcover, we're not trying to grow large plants. They need very little fertilizer to maintain good health because of their naturally slow growth. Pumping them full of fertilizer will create soft, watery growth, which is more disease prone. Let's look at which types of fertilizer to use.

Knowledge of a few nutrients essential to plants will make gardening more successful. Fertilizer labels give three numbers, which represent the percentage of nitrogen, phosphorus and potassium, always in that order, as N-P-K, the chemical element abbreviations. Generalizing, N, nitrogen, is for green leaf growth, but also for roots; P, phosphorus, is for root growth, and K, potassium, helps build strong stems, flower and fruit production. Already you can see that dwarf conifers and most groundcovers don't need a lot of leaf growth or fruit production, so choose a general purpose fertilizer with higher phosphorus for root growth, which is what the little plants need to survive drought situations.

A good all-purpose fertilizer label reads 5-10-5. In an inorganic (chemical) fertilizer rated 5-10-5, you're buying 80% filler with the nutrients as water-soluble salts: 5% nitrate, 10% phosphate, and 5% potash. For flowering shrubs and new plantings, 5-10-10 is a good choice. For all miniature plants, read the instructions for application amounts, then halve or quarter that amount, and water in well, which means to flood the soil twice after you work the fertilizer into the soil a bit. Be sure to allow the water to reach the bottom of the roots. Dig to test. Applying too much inorganic fertilizer or not watering well can chemically burn the roots; the top will wilt and probably die. Before you shop for fertilizers read below about organics and pH. Also check out Chapter 15, "Isolate your gardens from nuisance nibblers," which advises against inorganic fertilizer, if you want to repel browsing pests.

Other nutrients will get incorporated into your soil when you apply organic matter and crushed rock. Rock phosphate or bone meal are better sources of phosphorus (the middle number on fertilizer labels) because they are slow releasing and don't leach out of the soil, when watered, as readily as inorganic phosphates from salts. Organic matter in the form of composted leaves and shredded bark mulch is recommended over inorganic fertilizer, or in addition to it, for improving soil structure and adding micronutrients, which are needed in micro amounts by plants. Again, a little fertilizer goes a long way.

After the first season, spring feeding alone should be sufficient, with the exception of flowering shrubs, which need another summer application. Re-bloomers, like miniature roses and annuals, need still another application for more flowers. In early spring, feed established plants by side dressing around stems with granular fertilizer. Liquid fertilizer is fast acting, but leaches out readily. Slow-release fertilizer and organics are good, but require early application in spring, when soil is moist. Late applications encourage soft growth, which is easily attacked by insects and spider mites, when plants go somewhat dormant in summer. Fertilizer is wasted on dormant plants.

Soil structure and amendment

Without good soil structure, fertilizer won't help the plants. The size of granules in the soil must be balanced. Clay particles are the smallest and

During the hardscaping, PVC pipes were buried and connected to an irrigation valve and timer. The PVC was branched to five planting areas on Dave Stare's Dry Creek Railway. *Oak McCann photo*

The author sprays an anti-transpirant onto dwarf Japanese maple trees early in the morning to help them retain leaf moisture before a forecasted heat wave. *Oak McCann photo*

When groundcover invades the space of neighboring railroad track, cut away (divide) the groundcover with a knife or clippers and transplant the divisions into bare spots.

easily compacted into bricks when dry and muck when wet. It's too bad, because clay is full of mineral nutrients. Clay soil is heavy, prevents water penetration, once dry, and water runs off, so mix in sand while clay is moderately moist. Silt particles are mid-sized and sand is coarsest. Sandy soil is light, full of air, and poor in nutrients, which get washed away, because water percolates too fast. Usually it's difficult to find clay for sale, so enrich all soil types by incorporating organic matter.

Amendment with organic matter, fir bark, leaf mold, humus and well-composted manure act like a sponge to hold water between soil particles to make water-soluble nutrients available

to roots. A good rule of thumb is to mix two or three inches of organic material into the top 6-8" of soil when planting and continue to add an inch more as mulch every year around trees and shrubs and on the soil around groundcover. Finally, don't go overboard. It's better to incorporate organic matter into your existing soil (if it has no known toxins) than replacing it entirely with store-bought sandy loam with no clay, because soil with some clay chemically holds the nutrients.

Another rule of thumb is to keep slopes from exceeding 45 degrees to prevent soil erosion. Groundcover is only so effective at holding slopes against the force of falling rain and

runoff. Use rocks or retaining walls whenever possible to terrace slopes. It's difficult to grow all but the most xeric (dry-loving) plants on a steep slope.

Soil pH

Is your soil sweet or sour and why does it matter? Generally USA's east-coast soil is sour and west-coast soil is sweet, although salty would be more accurate. In scientific terms, soil that is sour or very acidic has a low pH and needs amendment in the form of ground oyster shells, limestone (calcium carbonate), or better yet, dolomitic limestone, which has magnesium as well. High pH soil is called alkaline or basic, usually due to a lack of water (rainfall) leaching out salts, as in arid land, the soil west of the plains states.

Most plants need soil to be slightly acidic, because at this range the water-soluble nutrients are available to the roots. Your local Cooperative Extension Service or a nursery expert can tell you about your soil type and what to do. Or you can get a pH meter at the garden store and amend the soil accordingly. Conifers and some evergreens, known as ericaceous plants, love more acidic soil, which is their natural habitat. Therefore if you're having trouble with yellowing conifers on the west coast, it could be that they aren't able to take up the fertilizer you're feeding them. Acidifying the soil a bit with fertilizers from the garden center may help. These fertilizers often say, "For azalea, camellia, and rhododendron." Conifer tree bark mulch will help, too. One way to avoid this problem is to plant native plants. The trend to plant natives is becoming more popular as retail nurseries make them available. In arid zones, alkaline loving plants from Australia's dry regions are rapidly filling the market.

Soil microorganisms

The unseen heroes in the garden are (or should be) the masses of microorganisms breaking down material as a by-product of their life process, making nutrients available to plants. Dead soil has none and it's difficult to produce anything in dead soil, but dead plants. When you plant your little 2" plants with 2" roots, they have almost two days' water resources at their disposal. Actually, most nurseries that sell dwarf trees use 2" pots that are 5" deep, just for this reason. Plants need to grow their roots as long and as wide as possible before summer's drying heat. A larger root system will prevent winter-drying damage, as well, and help to anchor the plant when frosts try to heave plants up out of the ground.

Microorganisms eat organic matter and can even form nodules on roots to help with absorption. No organic matter, no help. Too much undecomposed organic matter, like fresh wood chips, can cause all the microorganisms to stay busy breaking down the wood. Instead of helping the plants, they rob them. Fresh wood chips should stay above ground as mulch.

Recent exciting research with mycorrhizae shows that adding this fungus as an "inoculant" to soil before planting will double or triple the root mass of plants, because of the extensive tube-like system of fungus mycelia delivering nutrients to feeder roots. Unfortunately, applying some pesticides and disturbing the soil can kill existing mycelia. As recourse, work (inoculate) mycorrhizae into the soil around established plants with a trowel or spade. Fungi Perfecti® offers MycoGrow™ to reintroduce mycelia into the root zone where the symbiotic relationship helps the garden plants. See www.fungi.com/mycogrow/index.html

The nursery, Monrovia, feeds roots in their nursery pots. Their plant tag

Stem cuttings of 3-4" have been growing roots for several months in a kit-made greenhouse and will soon be transplanted out to the garden railway mountain to model a conifer forest.

Can you imagine a town with no children? Ed Assaf's healthy countryside has sprouted offspring from the surrounding parents. Ed propagated and transplanted three varieties of juniper, groundcover, and native mosses to show a natural blend of plants and color. A quarter of the trees on Ed's "Stretch of Track Between Here and There" are from cuttings.

advertises: "Our soil is alive... with microorganisms that maximize the disease resistance and fertility of your garden's ecosystem. Our custom soil blends are inoculated with life-enhancing mycorrhizae, natural [thread-like] fungus that strengthens root growth, improves nutrient absorption, and ensures better tolerance to transplant shock. ...Unlike most commercial soils, ours contains compost to help increase water reten-

tion and release precious nitrogen naturally." By upending the soil ball from the pot you will reveal the whitish colonies of mycorrhizae fungus.

Irrigation and water conservation

Again, we're trying to keep little plants little while they mature—slowly—and still get the required amount of moisture to them. New mini plants tend to have roots as deep as the tops grow

Weedy oxalis must be dug, not pulled, to remove long taproots. Pull them and root-like runners creep underground to make whole new plants with their own taproots. Leave them and they bloom cute little yellow flowers that fool you into keeping them (so their exploding seed capsules can cover your whole garden).

Labrador violets (*Viola labradorica*, Zones 3-9) started out as a sweet groundcover at the rear of the garden bearing purple flowers. Two years later exploding seed capsules invaded a neighboring field of once-tidy groundcover. These seedlings must be dug before it's too late. Applying a pre-emergent germicide will prevent a new invasion.

above the ground, so our mini gardens are challenged to find enough water on that fourth or fifth super-hot day without irrigation. Mulching the soil surface helps to prevent evaporation, as does incorporating mulch, as mentioned above. If you have elevated the garden above a retaining wall, unabsorbed water starts to drain out as soon as it's applied, making this the most critical of situations for incorporating sponge-like organic matter.

Knowing when to irrigate (add water) is also helpful. Early morning, before the sun comes up and breezes begin, is the optimum time to apply water. First, the water has time to be absorbed into the soil so plants are newly quenched during the hottest time of day. Second, the tops of plants dry off before the scorching sun's rays can use water droplets as prisms to blister leaves. Third, dry leaves are less prone to fungal disease, which is why night watering is not recommended. Finally, drip irrigation allows water to reach roots without wetting leaves. If too much mulch is applied, a drip system under the mulch will still allow water absorption, whereas spraying the mulch may prevent percolation into the soil below. Commonsense also tells us that if a plant is wilted, it is time to get water to it.

Anti-transpirants, like Cloud Cover™, sprayed on thin leaves cover them with a waxy coating that prevents excessive loss of moisture, which is constantly exiting the leaves on hot days. It also works in the winter to prevent cells from freezing on plants marginally susceptible to frost. Incorporate water-grabbing polymers into slopes to aid in water retention and give back moisture to soil roots when they need it. Please see Chapter 13, "Drought resistant plants and practices to reduce water usage."

Pests

Healthy plant cells make natural phyto-chemicals that resist attacks by insects and spider-like bugs. Too much water can create a haven for fungus and slugs, let alone a higher water bill. Too little water will create a haven for spider mites and sucking insects, which are easily washed away with a sharp stream of water from the hose. Prepare for times of excessive rain by properly pruning trees to keep them open to air and light. Weed and deadhead shrubs and groundcover to prevent spongy places where rot can take hold.

Control many sucking insects, like aphids, by spraying with a soap insecticide, which dries up bugs but doesn't hurt the environment. Because we're in such close proximity to our little plants while maintaining them and our trains on nearby tracks, organic

solutions prevent the worry of harming our families. Read Chapter 15, "Isolate your garden from nuisance nibblers" for more detailed suggestions and resistant plants.

Exposure

Drying winds, reflected heat from buildings, and prolonged, warm winter days are some of the problems that negatively affect plants. Check the tag for plant requirements. Conifers and other evergreens are especially susceptible to winter drying because their exposed leaves continue to transpire, but the roots may be frozen. Be sure they go into winter with enough stored moisture if the autumn has been dry, and then mulch the soil. Sensitivity to exposure in winter is in direct relationship to the plant's lack of hardiness. See Chapter 2, "Zoning laws for climate compatibility" and note the zones listed on charts in the large Part 3, "Plant Selection."

Adequate sunlight is needed to color conifers and other evergreens with yellow or white variegation, otherwise they revert to green. Flowering plants need light to initiate blooms. Too much shade can cause disease or lack of photosynthesis in certain plants. If your plants are stretching into spindly growth, looking for the sun, they could be hungry and unable to take up nutrients. Too much

7

When raising the grade around existing (1:1) trees, retain the new soil to create a well. Too high a grade piled onto roots can kill a tree. Wider trees require a wider well. Soil touching bark can damage or kill the tree. Note the weed-preventing landscape fabric where a trestle will be installed on Dave Stare's Dry Creek Railway.

Without strict rules, artists can create amazing plant sculptures. Manny and Veronika Neronha sculpted a tree and cascading shrubbery from one dwarf Japanese garden juniper. Be bold! Take hold of your pruning shears! Begin somewhere! Look to nature for models.

salt spray or road salt runoff can kill some plants, while others, like cryptomeria, corokia and juniper, are salt-resistant.

Transplant a $1 plant into a $5 hole

Many successful gardeners will say that the time to transplant is when you have the time and the potted plant is in your hand, ready to go. Ideally, give your transplants the best start possible so you don't waste time replacing them, jumping through hoops to nurse them back to health, or worse, leaving them languishing in sadness.

When you plan to plant an area, cultivate (dig) the soil and mix in some amendment at least two weeks prior to planting day. This establishes the microorganisms, thereby making nutrients available to new tender plants. It's like leaving your baby plants in the capable care of micro-babysitters while you're away.

In established gardens, always dig a hole for transplants that is three or more times as wide and a little deeper than the root ball (soil and roots below the stem). Mix a small amount of fertilizer or compost into the bottom of the hole, stir it around and cover it with a thin layer of soil so roots don't burn in direct contact with fertilizer.

Remember to halve or quarter the amount of fertilizer recommended on the label. Loosen the bottom roots, if

matted, and any that are wound around the root ball. Cut off extremely long roots that won't fit in the hole. Pull out and trim wrapped roots. Distressing the root ball is good! One of the primary reasons transplants don't make it is because roots never branch out beyond the pot size. Roots need help spreading out. Position the root ball so that its top is level with the top of the hole. Especially with conifers and ericaceous plants, do not cover the stem with soil or mulch, or it may rot. Do not expose the soil in the root ball to sun, which can kill soil mycorrhizae. Immediately backfill with amended soil, then water deeply and thoroughly. If the surrounding soil is very dry, first fill the hole with water, let drain, then transplant. By applying small amounts of fertilizer only under the plant, the surrounding soil grows fewer and weaker weeds, and roots get help growing down. It's important to water well and often the first few weeks. The above method is better than putting a $5 plant into a $1 hole.

Plant propagation

Briefly touching on this subject, if you know how easy it is to make several plants from one parent, you'll probably try it. After all, the plants are already multiplying, so helping to spread them around the garden is a cost-efficient and time saving practice. Increase the

quantity of new plants with one or more of five methods: seeds, cuttings, separation, division, and layering. Seeds will naturally create a root system and new leaves as part of the process, but the other methods require you to see that new plants have both roots to grow down and tops with growing points (buds). Some tops, like cranesbill, flatten out from one central undividable taproot and fool you.

Grasses and other bunching groundcovers need to be cut apart with a knife or spade. Transplant the divisions. The division process revives the mother plant, because dead material can be pulled out, and gives new plants space with new soil to grow in. Separation of clumps that just fall away from each other is similar to division. Bulbs, like chives and grape hyacinth, will separate.

Taking stem cuttings from the green wood (the last season's growth) of trees requires a little more knowledge of plant physiology to get roots to grow on the cut end. Water is the key, but air is needed, too. Sticking 2-4" short cuttings into a medium of moist sand, vermiculite, or perlite allows both air and water to initiate roots. Be sure to trim leaves cleanly off the bottom of stems so rotting leaves in the growing medium don't grow microorganisms that will attack the cutting. Mist tops or make cloches (mini greenhouses of

Judy Drake made a porous hypertufa bowl to edge the patio. Sedums and sempervivums in bright red say, "Stop!" creating a psychological barrier to the garden. Find out how to make your cement and aggregate containers at www.timpyworks.com/pamphlets/hypertufa-101/101.html.

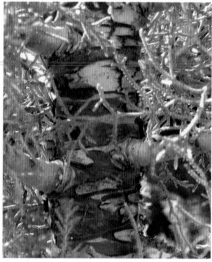

Bonsai artists value the bark on little trees almost more than the greenery. Of course, they go together like a horse and carriage, but excessive greenery needs to be carted away to make the bark visible. Here an intermediate-sized Arizona cypress (*Cupressus arizonica* 'Blue Pyramid', Zones 6-9) displays age and beauty in its peeling trunk. Pruning the fragrant leaves is aromatherapy.

Danny Saporito mows his mini lawns and edges them, too. The landscaping timber around his layout keeps the lawn edge easy to trim. All the little trees behind the houses are seedlings that Danny transplanted from his nearby woods. So far he's keeping up with the pruning.

plastic or glass) to prevent drying. Some gardeners create a whole forest of trees this way. Rooting hormone helps initiate roots, as does irrigation with a tea of water steeped with willow branches (natural hormones).

When is the best time to multiply and divide? During dormancy and after blooming are good times. Never disturb plants with tender growing points during active growth, as in spring. Early fall propagation allows plants to get established (anchored with new roots) before winter. Save seeds for spring planting or scatter in late fall for spring germination.

Layering is more advanced, but sprawling plants do it all the time. If you find a branch that has been buried and starts to root, the new plant can be excised from the parent and planted in its own space—it only needs roots and shoots. To "ground layer" a branch (also called serpentine layering), scrape an inch of bark from the under side of a stem at a node where you can bury it, hold it down with a rock or wire staple, and keep it moist. Rooting hormone powder applied to the exposed cambium layer just under the bark will help it along. Mark your calendar for two months then check for roots.

Weed abatement

Speaking of scattering seeds, some of the most aggressive weed pests are those with exploding seed capsules, like creeping woodsorrel (*Oxalis* sp.), which also spreads by runners. Their taproots must be dug, not just pulled, preferably before they set their little yellow flowers. If you don't want weeds in your garden, get them out of your neighboring lawn. Actually oxalis plants are quite small and almost cute, if you aren't aware that they are capable of taking over the whole garden. Not to single out oxalis as the only aggressive weed, this is just to expose new gardeners to the fact that weeds have several ways of spreading.

By allowing a few non-invasive natives, gardeners can relax a little about weeding. Scarlet pimpernel is a cheery little "weed" that doesn't elbow out our store-bought plants. It's your choice, as they're easily pulled. Allow space for this wildflower and then wax poetic with an ancient epithet, like, "No ear hath heard, no tongue can tell, the virtues of the pimpernel." See photo for its virtues.

The best way to rid your garden of incoming weed seedlings is to apply a pre-emergent germicidal agent, which

Scarlet pimpernel (*Anagallis arvensis*, Zones 6-10) is a non-invasive native, also known as poor man's weatherglass. At the approach of rain, it folds up its ¼" reddish-orange petals and keeps them folded on cloudy days.

Gary and Sue Robinson have been trimming two rockspray trees (*Cotoneaster microphyllus* 'Emerald Spray', Zones 5-9) for over 10 years. This one models a shrubby tree.

prevents seeds from sprouting. The toxic chemical pre-emergent, trifluralin (sold as Preen™) works, but turns brass rails blue and emits noxious fumes that make me worry about pets and family. A better choice is the pre-emergent made from corn gluten, safe enough to eat and even provides plant nutrients. Get Nature's Concern™ at better garden centers. Water into soil and repeat application after heavy rain.

I hesitate to recommend or even use landscape fabric for weed abatement, but it can be a knee and back-saver, once installed correctly in certain places. Heavy frost can heave it up in colder zones, so lay it deeply underground. Before installing walkways, roadbed, or trestle for railways, lay out the fabric and staple it down every foot or so with 6" long jute or irrigation wire "staples," which get hammered into the ground. Especially secure the edges, as there's nothing more like exposed underwear than plastic sheeting emerging from its grave. Leave at least 4 inches above it for the gravel, which needs to be tamped down. I don't recommend it under plants. Beware of pulling up deep-rooted weeds on edges as the fabric can be pulled up, too. See photo.

If weeds are too big to leave there, pull or dig them up. If they are too small to pull or dig, apply boiling water to kill them. Glyphosate (Roundup®) is not necessary and can devastate sensitive little plants, if carried on a breeze.

Edges, mulches and psychological barriers

Tidy edges say, "The day's work is done." Natural flagstone, whose appearance only improves with age, is one way to edge your garden and makes a good mow strip for the lawnmower. You can step on it to get into your layout and if there's a slope, you can lean it into the grade to create a soil-retaining wall.

Commercial edging material is effective, too, especially combined with a plant border. One friendly border is a low fragrant hedge, like rosemary or thyme, which smells heavenly as you lean over it to re-rail the train or dig that dandelion. A low hedge is a great way to tie together your garden elements.

While side dressing means applying fertilizer next to plants, top dressing either means fertilizing your lawn or dressing up the top of your soil with decorative mulches. When you're all done planting your new little garden and look out over a sea of brown with small green islands, you can wait years for the mature garden to fill it all in, or you can go to the landscape materials yard and buy some pebbles, cocoa mulch, sand (only if you have clay soil) and mini bark mulch to dress the bare soil.

In tiny gardens use one mulch over most of the garden, then contrast that with a river of another mulch, as long as the river fits the theme. At the base of mountains, the same colored rock in rough, rather than smooth, pebbles looks realistic. All mulches and top dressings will deter weeds.

More of a design concept than cultivation concern is the use of psychological barriers, which give viewers the signal to stay back and walk on paths, patios or lawn. Examples include edging material, potted plants, bright annuals, and low hedge borders. If you fully expect viewers to walk all over the garden railway and you don't want to post "walk here" and "don't walk here." signs, then help visitors navigate your empire with clearly identified walkways. The proverbial "yellow brick road" told travelers to Oz where to walk. You can make walkways equally as obvious with a common material, different than the garden's top dressings.

Mowing the groundcover

Chapter 18 lists 40 great low groundcovers, but eventually, too much kindness may make them billow up. If they start out low in the spring, the best time to trim them back is after they have bloomed or after they have hardened off at the beginning of summer and before it gets too hot. The best tool for this job is a battery-powered, hand-held weed and edging trimmer (keep your free hand out of the way). It's fast and accurate if you keep the blades parallel to the ground so that major stems don't get cut. String trimmers are okay for

The Robinson's second little rockspray tree was bought at the same time as the previous photo's and grown in a trough. Over the years, the branches have been trimmed to isolate shelf-like sprays of twigs so that the sun can reach and color all the berries bright pinky-red.

Without cultivation we can resort to native plants to model a scene. Native grassy brush appropriately serves the purpose on this stretch of Arizona Garden Railway Society's 7.5"-gauge railway.

taller groundcover, but they scatter the mess of cut material everywhere.

Some groundcovers emerge pristine in the spring and some look like they're having a permanent bad hair day by winter's end. Pull out or cut off any dead (brown and gray) leaves, and fill in bare spots with divisions from healthy areas just as soon as the ground can be worked in spring.

Tree trimming

One of the best times to prune trees for a scale appearance, or get them headed in the right direction, is before they get planted. Trim the plant on a table while you're seated and at eye-level with the work. Pruning trees before planting also lightens the load of the feeder roots, which will naturally be root-pruned during the stress of transplanting.

You can divide the pruning process into three bite-sized tasks:

1. At the root zone dig out any weeds, and expose the trunk a few inches by cutting off branches at the trunk anywhere from 2-6" from the soil, depending on the size of the tree and where you're locating it. Decide whether to make it a single trunk or multiple-stem trunk.

2. Clean any dead material from the branches or trunk. Unless you're a bonsai master, always trim off dead branches and pull out all dead leaves with a gloved hand. Remove any crossing branches and open the tree to the light and air by removing branches too

closely spaced. Branches should radiate out from the center.

3. Cut back the tips of wide branches always leaving a bud, not a stump, at branch tips. The overall profile, or habit of the tree, is a narrow triangle on conifers—either a symmetrical cone or an irregular leaning triangle. The top needs to have an apex and the bottom should be heavy with longer branches than those above them. Broadleaf trees often are pruned with more of a canopy, but still maintain the triangular profile. This is how to "age" a tree and keep it healthy.

For a more detailed account of pruning and a look at my favorite pruning shears, read Chapter 8, "Prune trees for a scale appearance."

Tools

Actually, most of the tools you use for regular gardening will be the same for miniature gardening, until you get to the pruning stage. Bonsai tools are handy for cutting the branches close to the trunk, but most pruning shears work fine. I use a titanium blade-honing tool (bonsai supplier) to keep my pruning shears sharp and cleaned of sap. Corona® makes a grape pruning clipper with curved by-pass blades, which cut branches close to the trunk. If you can find a child's plastic rake, that's what I prefer for cleaning up cut branches around groundcover, because the soft, flexible tines don't tear out the plants by the roots. I wear a fabric Fiskars®

belt pouch (not a stiff leather carpenter's belt) to carry the pruning shears (always pointed down in case I fall on it) and keep a collapsible kangaroo can (pictured in Chapter 8) nearby for trimmings. My most valuable tools are my $16 kneepads—I never work in the garden without them. Now get some flexible, water-resistant nitrile gloves (Atlas®, for example) that actually do fit like a glove and you're invincible. Better yet, buy half a dozen and keep them laundered for a truly pleasant gardening experience.

Save your plant tags. Later you can figure out which plants are best for your garden and buy more. You can read how to better care for them. Maybe one winter day you'll compile a notebook or journal and include them for reference.

7

Prune trees for a scale appearance

8

Have you ever visited a garden railway with realistic, scale-forest trees and wondered how they got that way? I recently visited such a railway with many groves of tall trees; each tree had proportionally way more height than width. These old-looking trees have spaces between the branches so we can admire the flaky bark of the trunks at intervals up the tree. Photo 1 shows a grove 15 years after planting 4"-high, rooted cuttings. If you've allowed your trees to become "Fat Alberts" and want to enhance realism, it's not too late.

1. Bob Evans bought many dwarf Alberta spruce trees as bare-root cuttings in 1994. He planted a grove and watched as his forest became a hedge over the years. Letting them grow tall allowed stout trunks to form. Finally, he found information on what to do and now keeps trees pruned on his Los Arabis Creek Railway.

In an effort to model conifer trees, garden railroaders usually go to the nearest garden center and find dwarf Alberta spruce shrubs. This classic, Christmas-tree-shaped evergreen has a nice, green color and a densely packed growth habit, giving it a fuzzy look. *Picea glauca* 'Conica' (aka. *P.g.* var. *albertiana* 'Conica') emerged onto the gardening scene when a pair of horticulturists waiting for a train noticed a "witches broom" growing on a white spruce in Alberta, Canada, 104 years ago. Every dwarf Alberta spruce since then is descended from that dense growth. The mature height in 10 years could reach five feet, or 10 feet in 20 years.

The following pruning discussion primarily deals with *P.g.* 'Conica'. There are smaller varieties, like *P.g.* 'Pixie' and *P.g.* 'Jean's Dilly', which I rarely prune and use as town and home trees.

I've been teaching clients to use the following technique, but I don't insist on it. Our garden railways are, after all, our personal thumbprints of expression. You might invent a better way, which I'd like to hear about.

The science

In a dozen years of visiting countless garden railways, I've found that the most-planted tree in just about any state, except in the deep South, is the dwarf Alberta spruce. Like Christmas trees, most are kept in a dense cone, perhaps cleaned of branches near the ground. Years pass. Although a true dwarf shrub, the tree's DNA creates a cone shape with a ratio of 2:1, height to width. They grow wider and wider, as they gain 2-4" in height each year. Recognizing this dilemma, some space-conscious railroaders get out the hedge clippers (and, yes, chain saws) to shear the sides and top, occasionally finding brown gaps when finished. This crew-cut treatment will keep the tree small only so long, because the sun-starved inside of the branch eventually runs out of growing points (buds). Dead gaps often appear the next year because the bud-filled tips have been removed, leaving older, non-productive tissue that won't sprout new growth.

The other issue is that shearing the tips makes the tree shrubbier and denser. The hormones in the tips say, "Oh yeah, cut off my terminal buds and I'll give you more buds—a lot more" (photo 2). The term for this is "pinching back." Call it

2. On his Ambitious & Tiring Railroad, a friend, Bob Fergusen, permitted the author to demonstrate pruning techniques on his dwarf Alberta spruce trees, all about 40" tall by 20" wide. The top of the tree in the foreground has been hacked off, revealing a dead spot inside, but the apex has lots of new growth.

what you like, it works only for a while; then you either have to like the dead look or replace the tree.

The timing

Before you run outdoors with magazine and pruners in hand, let's talk about when to prune. Dwarf Alberta spruce is recommended for USDA Hardiness Zones 3-8, but I've seen healthy specimens in Zones 9 and 10, given afternoon shade and enough water.

In warmer climates, I recommend severely pruning spruce in mid to late autumn so as not to stimulate a new flush of growth, which can be damaged by freezing temperatures. By cutting off bud-bearing branches at this time, you save yourself extra pruning next spring because buds are set on the previous years growth.

Alternatively, prune spruce trees just before or after their spring growth and before intense sun on hot days can burn newly exposed leaves. Some experts say fall pruning also has an advantage because summer pruning can expose new cuts to insect damage.

Those in the colder, northern climates need to prepare their plants for a longer dormancy, so fall pruning may send the wrong message (although I've seen recommendations for fall pruning of spruces in Zone 4). After the buds have sprouted and hardened (no longer tender), usually in May or June, a severe pruning in late spring will allow more time to repair for

The stronger, upper branchlet will be removed, leaving the weaker branchlet below. The cut will be made along the line of the lower rail.

3. To illustrate the pruning technique, this branch has been removed from the tree. The lower rail in the photo makes a nice, horizontal line to show where the author will prune that branch. Keeping the pruning shears horizontal prevents accidental cutting of other branches.

the coming winter. It's difficult to give advice for every situation in a book for an international audience, so I suggest you test your pruning skills on just a few trees before making a costly mistake. One or two dead trees can model lightning strikes.

The technique

Let's look at what to do if starting with a dwarf Alberta spruce that has been growing over five years in the ground (photo 2). In the photo, notice that a previous attempt to shorten the tree has produced lots of new growth around the dead apex; eventually this would make a bushy flat top. Even though I want to lower the apex, I start pruning at the bottom to see what the tree will tell me.

Spruce branches have what is termed an "opposite arrangement" of branches. Knowing this habit, I prune much of the growth away from the top of each branch, leaving a bottom "branchlet," and making sure that it has buds. To demonstrate this technique, I have placed a typical branch on a track in the orientation it was on the tree (photo 3). Opposite branchlets on the main branch point up and down, then left and right, and so on.

DNA tells the branch tips to point up, but there is a loophole, called "directional pruning." We want our lower branches to look heavy and old, and to point outward or perhaps down a bit. In photo 3, the lower rail shows the cutting path I will

The top of the tree has been removed and a stump left

This branch will form the new top of the tree

The branch has been bent vertically and tied to the remaining stump. When it has "remembered" its new position, the tie will be removed and the stump cut back.

4. Sap drips from the terminal cut at the top of the tree but it will soon heal. On its right, the new leader or apex will be tied snug to the stump.

5. Looking at the backside of the apex, we see the green twist-tie holding the lateral branch vertically against the top of the trunk, where the old top was removed. In a few weeks, when the apex remains vertical on its own, the stump will be cut off along with the tie.

take with my pruning shears on every branch of the tree, starting by pruning the strongest upward branchlet and leaving the weaker horizontal branchlet on the bottom. I'll then cut smaller branchlets off that one and finally cut the terminal end to eliminate the strongest, longest tips. I'll leave the shortest tips, with some buds.

Finding the place to start cutting is tricky on a densely branched shrub, as in the branch in photo 3. Pick a branch (any branch) and fold up only the tip to expose branchlets attached to that main branch. If you see a decent branchlet underneath, cut off the big one you are holding up (where it meets the branch). If, when you lift the remaining branchlet, you see another good branchlet underneath, cut off the one you're holding. Repeat this procedure on the entire tree, except the very top. If you see a cluster of branches coming off the trunk at one point, isolate a weaker one and get rid of the others. Less is more, but don't model a sparse mountaintop tree in a lush grove.

Decide at what height you want the lowest branches, based on the full-scale tree you are modeling, then similarly decide on the height of the tree. I leave low branches to hide things I find unsightly and remove them to expose goodies. Sometimes the plant will grow one or more secondary trunks and you may need to decide to keep one or part of one to hide a bare trunk on that side.

The apex

Lowering the top is not as difficult as you might think, but harder than just lopping off the top three years of growth, as happened in photo 2. There's a trick to it.

Using the tree's "apical dominance," choose a good-looking side branch a few inches lower than the intended top. Pick a lateral branch on the side of the tree you call the front. Unless you waited about 10 years too long, this branch will be flexible and you can bend it up, snug to the trunk.

In photo 4, I've chosen the branch on the right and cut off the top of the tree to leave an important, but temporary, stump. Photo 5 shows the placement of a temporary (green) twist-tie. Be sure to remove the tie and the stump after the branch has retained the "memory" of its new verticality. Having pruned hundreds of little trees, I occasionally find apices on which I forgot to remove the tie and find that a bulging gall has formed under the tie, while other branches have assumed dominance. This can be fixed using the above technique.

Aesthetic pruning

Finally, in photo 6 we see the results of a half hour of pruning the tree in the center. I decided to begin the bottom branches only 4" from the ground to hide the street. In the process of pruning, I relieved the tree of two-thirds or more of its growth, not to mention the dead leaves piled up inside with snails, spiders, and a peanut hidden by a jay. Inside branches will be happy to receive the wind, sun, and rain, which will help keep the tree healthy. Spray it with the hose to repel the notorious spider mites during hot spells.

We garden railroaders are actually pioneers in this process of creating scale trees in our gardens. However, we can learn from the bonsai masters and from the tree itself. This method of pruning translates to many conifer species. Because we're

6. One down … now to clean up the branches. The top has been lowered only a few inches, by choice, but the tree has been reduced many inches on the sides. Note the shelf-like position of the branches.

growing plants in the ground, our trees usually have more vigorous root growth than those in pots, helping us achieve greater success.

It may help to have a professional person start the process, which you can then more easily maintain. Such was the case in photo 1, in which a person who had taken a course in "Aesthetic Pruning" got the homeowner past the initial severe pruning so he could then keep them in scale. If you want to experiment, prune a few trees when you feel like it, then see what they do. Get your gloves on!

9

Annuals for color and contrast

1. Parrot's beak lotus pours on the steam all summer producing bright orange-red blooms, contrasted with blue green feathery foliage. Draped over an exquisite travertine-tile portal this annual ensures that we'll notice the details on Richard and Melinda Murray's Green Hills Railroad long after the trains go away.

Annuals sometimes have trouble getting respect among "serious" garden railroaders because of their showy blooms and look-at-me flair. But we can use their showmanship to advantage. Because annuals are plants that live only one year, they are genetically designed to produce seeds for offspring, so we can count on them to bloom all summer, or at least until they do their job of producing seed. Deadhead them and feed them if they stop blooming. Place these attention getters where they will highlight a nice feature as above in photo 1, and they'll do the pointing for us, keeping us slyly humble.

2. Lee and Joan Sampson have allowed the seeds of sweet alyssum to "self sow" all over their garden railway. Even on this rainy day, it's a happy sight.

3. David and Judy Drake's Chickadee Western relies on the help of bright impatiens flowers to keep foot traffic off the railroad tracks.

4. Brian and Shirley Wenn positioned a grouping of moss rose next to a footbridge lit by a landscape light. Notice individual moss rose plants scattered throughout the garden, which integrate the scene.

It's quite obvious at the bottom of photo 2 that not all annuals are too showy or too large. The tiny flowers of sweet alyssum create a groundcover to rival any thyme. Where larger blooms exceed your standards for shrubbery next to buildings and little figures, place them at your feet. Showstoppers, like impatiens in photo 3, tell us it's time to stop and watch the train go by. Although it's low, this is a psychological barrier and obviously not a foot-path. On a similar mission in photo 4, a clump of moss rose plants in every color calls attention to the walkway it flanks. Small patches of moss rose carry the colorful theme into the railway where bright boxcars vie for attention.

Annuals come in hard-working foliage plants, too. Alternanthera (photo 5) loves full sun, and coleus (photo 6)

5. Joseph's coat and sessile joyweed are two alternantheras that explode with color all summer.

6. Coleus plants are usually seen with huge leaves in shady gardens. Keep this Tiny Toes where it's feet stay moist, but it can take some sun as well.

7. Marigolds and begonias light up the far side of Bob and Marlene Shore's north-of-the-border Shoreline Rail Road during a late evening train run.

Annuals with small features

Common name	Botanical name	Size	sun/shade	Description, comment	Zones
Joseph's coat, sessile joyweed	*Alternanthera sessilis*	8"x8"	sun/pt. sh.	red shrubby foliage, moist soil	10-11
Wax begonia	*Begonia* x *semperflorens-cultorum*	12"x12"	sun/pt. sh.	lustrous broad leaves, waxy flowers	8-11
English daisy	*Bellis perennis*	6"x8"	sun/pt.sh.	rose, pink or white flowers, biennial	3-8
Cornflower	*Centaurea cyanus* 'Dwarf Blue Midget'	6"x8"	sun	silver foliage, true blue flat flowers	na
Dahlberg daisy, golden fleece	*Dyssodia tenuiloba*	6"x4"	sun/pt. sh.	fine foliage, ½" gold daisies, fragrant	10-11
Hip Hop spurge	*Euphorbia* 'Hip Hop'	8"x12"	sun/pt. sh.	mounds of tiny white flowers on green	10-11
Impatiens, busy Lizzy	*Impatiens* 'Super Elfin Mix'	10"x12"	sun/shade	mounds, pinwheel flowers, takes shade	na
Edging lobelia	*Lobelia erinus* 'Riviera Mix'	6"x10"	sun/pt.sh.	blue, lavender, pink or white flowers	9-11
Sweet alyssum	*Lobularia maritima* 'Easter Bonnet'	4"x6"	sun/pt. sh.	white, pink, purple flowers, fragrant!	9-11
Sweet alyssum	*Lobularia maritima* 'Easter Basket Mix'	4"x6"	sun/pt. sh.	white, pink, purple flowers, fragrant!	9-11
Parrot's beak lotus	*Lotus berthelotii* 'Amazon Sunset'	6"x12"	sun/pt. sh.	fine leaves, red beaked flowers, moist	9-11
German chamomile	*Matricaria recutita*	10"x8"	sun/pt.sh.	daisy-like flowers, fine foliage	na
Moss rose	*Portulaca grandiflora*	6"x 6"	sun	succulent in all colors but blue	na
Fanflower	*Scaevola* 'Mauve Clusters'	4"x24"	sun	lavender fan-shaped flowers, spreads	10-11
Coleus, painted nettle	*Solenostemon scutellarioides* 'Tiny Toes'	6"x8"	sun/pt. sh.	colorful foliage mound, moist soil	na
Bacopa	*Sutera cordata* 'Bridal Showers'	6"x36"	sun/pt. sh.	white (pink, blue) flowers, moist soil	9-11
Glory plant, bacopa	*Sutera cordata* 'Gold 'n' 'Pearls'	6"x12"	sun/pt. sh.	chartreuse leaves, white flowers	10-11
Marigold	*Tagetes signata* var.	8"x8"	sun	fine foliage, orange to gold flowers	9-11

Zones are USDA Hardiness Zones, na= plants are non-hardy annuals Size is height by width, Sun is 5 or more hours per day of direct sun. Pt.sh.=partial shade

loves part shade. Both love moist soil. Red leaves blaze all summer and their tiny flowers are inconspicuous.

While you're waiting for perennial groundcovers or slow-growing shrubs to spread, it's a good idea to keep the soil covered to prevent weeds from taking over.

Annuals will be glad to accommodate. Those gardeners who have to wait until July for summer will appreciate the chart "Annuals with small features" for quickly coloring railroads or filling bare spots in rock gardens. Although one northern family (photo 7) had a beautifully mature railway garden, I was

8. Every year, sky blue lobelia is incorporated next to Jim and Jackie Ditmer's Osaka and Orient Express water feature, representing embankment shrubs. Bottom right, bacopa spreads over rocks with white flowers on trailing stems.

9. Hip Hop spurge is new this year. Hmmm … nice little leaves and flowers. What will it look like in my garden?

10. Jim and Pam Greer's Pine Needle Railroad found a way for a pot to upstage the begonia on their whimsical and fun-filled layout.

also attracted to a corridor way in the rear where orange trains picked up the color of marigolds lighting up a dark space in the evening.

Blue is hard to find and doesn't seem to last long enough on perennial plants. Lobelia saves the day with a variety of blues to choose from (photo 8). While some of us are looking forward to the day when we won't have to get more plants to fill in the garden, some of us love to find that new plant (photo 9) and bring it home for a while. How will it do? Will it get along with the other plants? It's fun to change up our gardens every year with a few little annuals.

Annuals are the party plants. Unabashedly they'll try to steal the show whenever possible (photo 10).

10 Aquatics have wet feet

All in submerged pots, palm-like dwarf papyrus and the low, water clover on the left, along with parrot's-feather stems (right), soften the rocky pond edge of Don and Marilyn Pickett's Danville, Alamo & Little Creek Railroad.

Ah, summer. It's hot enough for iced tea and watermelon. You're sitting by your little pond, enjoying the rhythmic chimes of rushing water from your railway's beautiful falls. Through the haze your eyes rest on a serene lake; you're imagining that anticipated fishing trip. Mountains reflected in cool, clear water ... but wait—the water's slimy green and what is all that stringy stuff? Awakened from your reverie, you put down the watermelon and reach into the water to bring out an unappetizing rake-full of algae accompanied by who-knows-what little creatures, wiggling as in a bad dream. Huh?

At the other end of the Picketts' pond, dwarf cattail simulates rushes while sessile joyweed brightens the foreground in a mass of red leaves.

Instead of wishing you had invested in a finished cellar for your railroad, let's look at environmentally friendly alternatives. Just as we have learned how to care for our locomotives, track, and trees, our water features require maintenance and sometimes retrofitting.

Keep the pond and grow plants that do some of that maintenance for you or, as a revolutionary new concept, create a "pondless" water feature!

After I show you how some folks have used aquatic plants successfully we'll look at how to fill that pond for an easy, easy water feature.

It's alive!

A healthy and attractive water feature is a complex living organism that responds to the elements just as we do. Without a virtual glass of iced tea to cool it down, the pond needs other helpers. Get solutions through online nurseries, like *www.ponds plantsandmore.com*. Find out how barley straw controls algae at *http://ohioline.osu. edu/a-fact/0012.html*. What I learned is that 40-50% of a pond's surface needs to be covered with plants to keep it crystal clear without chemicals. Plants gobble up undesirable nitrates and ammonia from fish and debris. Some plants oxygenate. Photosynthesis results in the oxygenation

of water, and microorganisms that use up excess nutrients, so don't fertilize your aquatics if you have algae "bloom." Three groups of plants do the trick.

Floaters for shade. Keeping water temperatures down also keeps algae down. With a floating canopy of plants that simulate lily pads, you are providing the most desirable help. Floaters shade the water and fish, use up nutrients before algae can get started, don't require planting, and settle easily back to normal after wildlife skirmishes involving marauding raccoons.

Submerged potted aquatics. Leaves float but roots and stems live underwater,

Greening the stream of the pondless water feature on Jerry and Alison Ogden's Possum Creek Railroad are clumps of dwarf golden sweet flag and corkscrew rush in a bonsai planter next to the dock.

Jerry and Shirley Bradley's retrofitted pondless waterfall on their Indigo Mountain Railroad. The island is a feather-rock planter with dwarf yaupon holly (*Ilex vomitoria* 'Nana,' Zone 7-10) and dwarf Japanese juniper (*Juniperus procumbens* 'Nana,' Zone 4-9) covering the plant-pot reservoir housing the pump under some filter material.

Water plants for the garden railway

Common name	Botanical name	Description	Zones
Without soil or pots			
Water fern, fairy moss	*Azolla caroliniana*	Tiny, floating "ferns"	7-10
Duckweed	*Lemna minor*	Smallest floating plants	6-10
American frogbit*	*Limnobium spongia*	Floating, spreads rapidly	7-10
Mosaic plant*	*Ludwigia sedioides*	Floating, tiny green diamonds	9-10
Watercress*	*Nasturtium officinale, N. microphyllum*	Shade OK, oxygenating, edible	4-11
Potted plants below water level			
Sessile joyweed*	*Alternanthera sessilis*	Spreading, brilliant magenta leaves	9-11
Dwarf umbrella palm	*Cyperus alternifolius* 'Gracilis'	2' high palm-like clumps	7-11
Dwarf papyrus	*Cyperus papyrus* 'King Tut' or 'Nana'	18" high "palms," some shade OK	9-11
Chamaeleon plant	*Houttuynia cordata* 'Variegata'	Colorful leaves, plant in shallow water	5-10
Corkscrew rush	*Juncus effusus spiralis*	Green, wiry corkscrews, shade OK	4-10
Water clover	*Marsilea minuta, M. quadrifolia*	Floating four-leaf-clover leaves	6-11
Forget-me-not*	*Myosotis scirpioides*	Tiny, baby-blue flowers in spring	3-10
Dwarf parrot's feather*	*Myriophyllum brasiliensis* var. 'Spiralis'	Oxygenating, spreading, feathery	6-10
Little floating heart*	*Nymphoides peltata, N. cordata*	Mini lily pads, small yellow flowers	5-10
Bald cypress	*Taxodium distichum*	Woody, deciduous conifer tree	4-10
Dwarf cattail	*Typha minima*	Tiny cattails, one-foot grassy leaves	4-9
Marginal and bog plants in moist soil			
Dwarf variegated sweet flag	*Acorus gramineus* 'Pusillus Minimus Aureus'	Shade OK, 4" yellow iris-like leaves	5-11
Bugleweed	*Ajuga reptans* 'Chocolate Chip'	Some shade OK, bog OK	3-9
Dwarf elephant ear	*Colocasia fallax* 'Silver Dollar'	4-6" showy leaves like shade	7-10
False heather	*Cuphea hyssopifolia*	Blooming trees along banks	9-11
Stargrass	*Dichromena colorata*	Some shade OK, top of soil out of water	7-10
Dwarf scouring rush, horsetail	*Equisetum scirpoides*	Non-invasive, in-scale rushes	4-10
Creeping Jenny	*Lysimachia nummularia* 'Aurea'	Mat forming, yellow flowers	4-8
Hosta	*Hosta* sp.	Stemless, heart-shaped shade lovers	3-9

*Invasive and restricted in some states

anchored in gravel or potted in soil topped with gravel to prevent the soil from muddying the water. Raccoons can have some fun with these less stable plantings, but I've seen a solution in the form of a low, electrified, one-wire fence, barely noticeable and hooked to a battery.

Pretty perimeter plants. Marginals (so-called by nurseries) and bog plants live at water's edge, barely submerged in pots hidden with stones or in moist soil. This group is so diverse that it includes just about any plant you might fancy, from colorful to carnivorous. In the wild we find some very-large-leaved marginal plants, like gigantic Gunnera, shocking us with rhubarb-shaped leaves bigger than we are. As modelers we can take advantage of this fact and grow larger, leafy plants in the foreground of the pond and make distant plants appear smaller by contrast. Here, taller grassy plants shade the water and call attention to the habitat, differentiating it from other plantings.

Go pondless!

Several years ago I first saw a waterfall emptying into what looked like a field of wet pebbles. Where was the water going? Turns out, there was a substantial hole in the ground lined with pond-liner material or a ready-shaped pond from a home-improvement store. I now use 60- to 100-gallon stock troughs from a feed store. Like nature's streams, the "pond" is filled with pebbles, large on the bottom, small on top. Reserve an area for the pump so that access is easy. Reservoirs for pumps can be purchased at pond stores or homemade from plant pots. As the water filters through the stones it enters the pump clean, ready for the falls, with no algae to scoop. As with other water features, the pump needs to run 24/7 for aeration, or helpful microorganisms will die and create malodorous fumes.

Since learning of this pond alternative, I've helped to build several pondless water features to minimize maintenance. Concerned about the cost of running large pumps all the time, I've installed a second, smaller pump alongside the big one to aerate the water at night. Pumps alternate duty via automatic timers. Aquatic plants can still be submerged in pots below pebble level to give the effect of water. "Float" a rowboat on the water-sprayed pebbles. Now you can run trains.

Ask the masters

Question: Which plants have you found best for your water features?

Patience Hoag
Phoenix, Arizona, Zone 10
I've got a couple of plants that do well right next to our waterfalls and ponds. One is English ivy, a trailing groundcover, and the other is a purple-colored morning glory (*Ipomea*), which is really spectacular in the spring. There is also a tropical-looking dwarf umbrella palm that voluntarily spreads to different areas around the water feature. Our success with these plants in the desert may be because the two waterfalls on our railway are under big shade-cloth awnings.

Ray Turner
San Jose, California, Zone 9
I have a small stream feeding a mill and millpond, with a sluice running water to the wheel. Next to it grows a false heather that seems to thrive. I have to prune it heavily to keep it looking like a tree rather than a big bush. All spring and summer it has small, purple flowers.

Jan Schreier
Minnetonka, Minnesota, Zone 4
As founder and current editor of the newsletter for the Minnesota Water Garden Society (*www.mwgs.org*), I've found a few water plants that are in scale with the garden railroad.

The smallest are fairy moss, duckweed, and American frogbit. These float on top of the water, helping to shade the water and compete for nutrients with algae. They work well only when the water is not moving, as in a container garden or in a small, still pond. Since they multiply rapidly, you'll be scooping them out of the pond regularly, which makes it great for sharing or composting.

Frogbit leaves mimic water-lily pads without blossoms. Mix this with miniature Japanese sweet flag (which looks like miniature iris leaves) along the edge of the pond, and you have just

Trailing vines of English ivy and morning glory green the banks of Dan and Patience Hoag's water feature in Phoenix. *Dan and Patience Hoag photos above and below*

Dwarf umbrella palm sprouts in clumps around the Hoags' Eaglewings Railroad.

created an in-scale Monet painting next to your railroad.

Other water plants have foliage small enough to look like in-scale cattails or pampas grasses. A favorite is the miniature cattail, which grows 12-18" tall. It is barely hardy in my Zone 4 garden and actually needs a cold winter dormancy to form its round catkins. A great waterside plant with miniature foliage and a tight,

well-behaved habit is the miniature horsetail (*Equisetum scirpoides*), growing to 8" tall. Don't confuse this with the water horsetail (*E. fluviatile*), which is an equally lovely scale plant, but which will jump the pond and you will be forever pulling it out of all places with damp soil. The good news is that it doesn't grow in dry soil and it can be readily sheared like to keep it less wild-looking.

10

A little false-heather tree shades the sluice at Ray and Ellen Turner's Mystic Mountain Railroad. *Ray and Ellen Turner photo*

Sue Piper's thyme-draped stream. *Sue Piper photo*

container. For a more dramatic effect at greater cost, try the 'Black Magic' cultivar, with dark-purple leaves that can reach five feet in height (or the smaller 'Silver Dollar'), obtained from a mail-order supplier like Wayside Gardens (*www.waysidegardens.com*).

Dick Friedman
Sacramento, California, Zone 9

Around my pond I've tried to grow a number of plants, using the water in the pond as well as nearby drip irrigation. The small reed-like plants didn't last past the first year. I've substituted ajuga around one side. It covers the ground and keeps weeds out. It's not to scale, but I like it. If I had it to do over again, I might use "chocolate chip" ajuga for the smell alone!

On the other side of the pond (the farm) I wanted to plant alpine strawberry, with small leaves and berries the size of peas. No one had it, so I planted several large strawberry plants. They're not to scale, but cover the ground and provide food when working in the garden!

Sue Piper
San Diego, California, Zone 10

We love the sparkle and sound created by the streams and waterfalls in our railroad and only turn them off when we are going to be away from home for more than a couple of days. Because we use chlorine tablets to eliminate problems with algae, we do not have any plants actually in the water.

We have had good success with Elfin thyme (*Thymus serpyllum* 'Elfin', Zone 4-10) planted along the banks of our lava-rock stream. The porous rock provides a secure foothold for the happily cascading plants and the thyme is tolerant of any heat absorbed by the rocks in the summertime. The profuse, tiny pink blooms are a glorious bonus.

Bill Hewitt
Mansfield, Massachusetts, Zone 5

I have poor luck with plants in my pond because it's in a poor location for sunlight, but I can grow a few water lilies. To line the waterfall and stream, I like hosta, which gives a nice effect along the border, simulating trees along a stream.

Herb Zuegel
Near Chicago, Illinois, Zone 5

Consider "Elephant ears." The *Colocasia* family, as it's properly called, is great and showy on the margins of a water feature. Here in Zone 5 it's best to grow them in a tub that can be brought to the basement for dormancy during the winter. In Zone 7 and warmer climates they can probably stay outside. *Colocasia* grows easily from sweet-potato-like tubers simply buried in warm, sloppy soil. Asians eat these roots, which a Chinese friend calls "Taro." As an inexpensive experiment, I bought several in his ethnic food store and have grown this green-leaved variety successfully for some years. By occasionally using water-soluble plant food, they've formed a nice 12"-wide by 12"-high clump in an old watertight

11

Cascading trees and the rocks that support them

Supported by the vertical rock on the left and cantilevered rocks on the right, three railway lines run almost directly over one another. A blue atlas cedar grows on the top terrace and hangs over the middle terrace. Two threadleaf Japanese maples cascade over the waterfall on Jim and Jackie Ditmer's Osaka & Orient Express.

Relaxing on our patio, controller in hand, we appreciate our cascading, story-telling little trees. Draped over the rock retaining wall cliff, inverted trees reach down to a train as it carefully maneuvers a curving ledge below. Bearing the weight of winter snow or even avalanches and rock falls, one tree trunk grows downward, and the branches respond by finding their place in the sun. Gazing up at a cliff face, we discover a mature and healthy tree, but its falling angle betrays a tortured past. How to portray these remarkable circumstances and make them look natural is the topic of this chapter.

The top of a waterfall is the perfect mirror image for this Irene prostrate rosemary at Don and Marilyn Pickett's Danville, Alamo & Little Creek Railroad.

On Jerry and Alison Ogden's Possum Creek Railroad, all three types of rock-wall construction allow an upper line to pass nearly above the lower line: vertical rocks at the base, concave in the center, and stacking on either side. A young juniper will someday arch the track.

I'd like to show you how woody trees, growing at odd angles, will tie together elements of your garden railway by allowing your eye to follow their lead. Cascading and leaning trees act as pointers to draw viewers into a story that is both unusual and perfectly natural. Sometimes we fret when our straight-as-an-arrow conifers share space with a rebellious, not-quite-vertical cousin, as if nature has that kind of perfection as a goal. I find that nature is restorative and makes its own corrections that are every bit as wondrous as hundreds of tall trees, seemingly parallel to each other.

Training for balance and proportion
I joined a bonsai club for a few years. Each week I brought to class a different one-gallon nursery can with a foliage mass aspiring to be a tree. I practiced hands-on techniques to transform a bush into a miniature tree. While occasionally wiring branches using specially annealed (softened) wire, I also learned how to pick nursery stock with well-spaced branches, an aged trunk, and the start of a shape I wanted. I recommend getting some help. You will be amazed at how learning a few principles goes a long way. With a little judicious pruning, we will be able to see the bark at several places along the trunk, an essential component of a tree as opposed to a shrub.

Armed with information, your time will be wisely spent, even if you make the inevitable mistakes. Fear not: meticulous precision is not necessary, although one

Hardscape suggestions for cascading trees on a steep grade

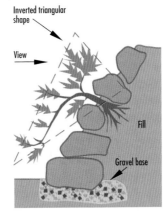

Figure 1. Stacking boulders

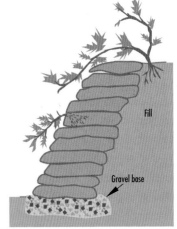

Figure 2. Stacking flagstone or ledger

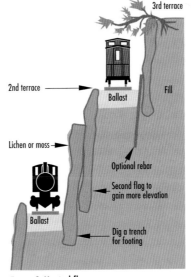

Figure 3. Vertical flagstone

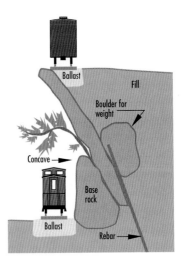

Figure 4. Cantilevered flagstone

Illustration by Marc Horovitz

As it leans over the pond, a short-needled atlas cedar seems to point the way for Bruce Sherman's live-steam C-21 on Richard and Melinda Murray's Greenhills Railroad.

Recommended plants for cascading trees in your railway

Common Name	Botanical Name	Description	Zone
Threadleaf Japanese maple	*Acer palmatum dissectum* var.	deciduous, colorful fall leaves	5-9
Blue atlas cedar	*Cedrus atlantica* 'Glauca'	bluish, short-needled conifer	6-9
Turkish cedar	*Cedrus libani* var. *stenocoma*	bluish short-needled conifer	5-9
Dwarf Hinoki cypress	*Chamaecyparis obtusa* 'Nana'	dark green, slow-growing conifer	4-8
Streib's Findling cotoneaster	*Cotoneaster dammeri* 'Streib's Findling'	broadleaf evergreen, weeping	4-9
Littleleaf cotoneaster	*Cotoneaster microphylla* 'Thymifolius'	evergreen apple tree look	4-9
Blue Stripe juniper	*Juniperus communis* 'Blue Stripe'	low, spreading conifer	3-7
Japanese juniper	*Juniperus procumbens* 'Nana'	classic, easiest cascading conifer	4-9
Kurume azalea	*Rhododendron* sp. kurume type	thirsty, colorful blooms, brittle	7-10
Prostrate rosemary	*Rosmarinus officinalis* 'Irene'	easy but needs much pruning	8-10
Boyd's creeping willow	*Salix repens* 'Boyd's Pendula'	pussy willow, pendulous	4-7
Cole's prostrate hemlock	*Tsuga canadensis* 'Cole's Prostrate'	tiny-needled conifer, shade OK	3-9
Dwarf Chinese wisteria	*Wisteria sinensis* 'Kofuji'	deciduous, pendulous purple flowers	5-8

Tip: "procumbens or prostrata" indicates a horizontal growth habit.

could make a therapy session of this art. Wire is not necessary either, but may quicken the desired results. The best bet is to find a how-to book, like *Bonsai Basics* by Pessey & Samson, or buy an ebook at *www.bonsaigardener.org*. With a few step-by-step lessons, you can branch out of verticality.

If you are adventurous, I can get you started with a capital "S." A straight-stemmed young tree can be planted at an angle, wired into an "S," and weighed down with lead fishing weights, heavy bolts, or the like until the trunk gets a "memory" of its new shape in a month or so. A curving trunk is more pleasing to the eye, as is a curving stream: accentuate the positive by growing branches on the out-side curves and eliminate material from the inside curves. Remove the wire as soon as you can to prevent it cutting the bark. Sometimes I'll find a nursery plant grow-ing on its side, so that the trunk is leaning over the edge of the pot and is curved already. This is a great start.

Branches, like shelves, need space between them—enough for a scale bird to fly into to perch. I clean foliage from above each branch by pinching or snipping it down to the branch to reveal the web-like twig pattern. Its overall triangular shape will now be reversed so that the apex at the bottom of the plant has shorter branches than the top, root end (figure 1). Because nutrients best flow upward in the trunk, take care to see that this style gets fed properly. Conifers, like junipers, will not mind being watered every day, but watch maples and azaleas for drying.

Rocks support the scene
In order to show off your cascading trees, they need elevation. Along with herba-ceous trailing vines, cascading trees soften a mass of rock by greening the rock wall and adding living texture.

Stacked-rock wall. While building a retaining wall of boulders, leave a space for planting a little tree "falling" out of the cliff at a 45-degree angle (figure 1). Mulch the soil around roots with fibrous moss to pre-vent erosion around the roots and subse-quent drying out (See Sharon and Bob Yankee's tip in "Ask the masters.") Stack-ing either flat flagstone or blocky ledger (figure 2) creates many pockets for plant-ing and breaks up the usual boulder look. Stacked-rock walls need to be built so that

Ask the masters

Question: What are your woody-stemmed plant choices for portraying cascading (falling) and leaning trees in your garden railway?

Doug Matheson
Manotick, Ontario, Zone 4
I garden mainly in the shade in a cold-climate environment so there are few woody cascading plants available. The only reliable conifer that will grow in the shade is hemlock. It is normally a large forest tree, but using bonsai techniques (and more patience than most of us have), it can be trained in a slanting style. If the shade is very light, yews are also a good choice and easily shaped. My favorites for cascading in full sun are of course the junipers, which come in a wide variety of colors, from golden through deep green.

Sharon and Bob Yankee
Mulino, Oregon, Zone 7
Our experience with cascading and leaning trees has been with Japanese garden juniper, Green Mound juniper, and the slow growing hemlock, Cole's Prostrate. These plants will drape nicely

over banks, rocks, or anything near them for support. Both junipers are fast growing so do best in a sunny location where quick evergreen cover is needed (read that as three to four years). They will both make a beautiful living tunnel if you plant two of the same variety and let them grow together. The tunnel can be kept open by either diligent trimming or placing the plants over a wooden frame or large pipe.

Cole's hemlock, which prefers a shady location, will creep along the ground or will make a beautiful draping effect over rocks or cliffs. It can be used in smaller spaces. Cole's hemlock and the mini willow, Boyd's Pendula, can be staked and tied to grow upward, then let cascade down. In two to three years the stake can be removed. For leaning trees, the smaller cotoneasters such as Himalayan Dwarf, Streib's Findling, or Thymifolia can be planted at an angle when young, then trimmed to reflect the leaning tree shape.

We have also had interesting results with the dwarf Alberta spruce, Jean's Dilly, by planting it horizontally into a mountainside. It will naturally curve

Tunnel of two junipers on the Yankees' line. *Sharon and Bob Yankee photo*

upward in a year or so. We call these "cliff hangers." When planting the cliff hangers, we suggest placing the water-grabber polymers deep in the planting hole to help retain moisture, as plants will not receive water in the usual way. Be sure to follow the directions on the polymers carefully. Too much, and they will thrust the plant out of the hole. We speak from experience!

each layer is recessed a bit into the hill for stability. This angle helps to prevent rocks from shifting and falling during frost heaves or heavy rain.

Vertical cliff. What if you lack the space because of a small yard or the need for a large radius track for long rolling stock? I find the easiest wall-like cliff is made by digging a narrow trench, where you want the grade to rise steeply, and inserting lichen-covered flagstone to lean slightly against the grade or hill (figure 3). A row of these rocks with the top edges at the same grade looks like the mountain was cut away for the railroad. Erosion is contained with a minimum of land lost to gain elevation. A great feature of a vertical-rock wall is the opportunity to run track above a lower line. For even more space, try the next treatment.

Concave cliff. On a hike along a back road, have you ever looked up at a cantilevered cliff? Trees on rock faces jut out

and seem to hang in limbo over your head. Engineering strength into cantilevered cliffs permits planting of trees on top or under the top edge. Start with a heavy boulder at the base of the slope (this rock you will see). Lean a large, thick flagstone against the far side of the base rock and weigh it down with another heavy boulder on the opposite side of the flagstone. Then pound in some half-inch or thicker rebar rods next to the flag to prevent it from tipping over. Fill behind the flagstone with soil for planting your cascading tree or ballast for the train (figure 4). Repeat for a longer concave cliff.

Now you've gained ground both horizontally and vertically and prevented the dreaded erosion from washing away your micro world.

Green "waterfalls"
As if frozen in time, a downward-flowing composition of branches shows move-

ment without motion. Its twisted trunk models the action and grace of a cascading stream. Even if you model a rock fall instead of a water feature, the element of a cascading tree will help to tell the story of a tree also fallen yet still thriving.

What will your tree point to … a cool brook floating a raft and fisherman, a hiker scaling rugged rocks, a rusting locomotive wreck? Curiously enough, one bonsai sensei (teacher) suggests that the bonsai tree will begin to reflect the mind of the cultivator, gradually taking on the very character of that person. Sounds like the ultimate adventure for a gardener! Another sensei says to let nature be your mentor as you discern what feels harmonious and bring it into form. All agree that our miniature trees, leaning or upright, are not mere objects but a process, not a goal but representative of the interdependence of all phenomena. I just think it's fun!

11

12 Deserts need succulents

Smoke from the cliffs signals the end of the run for Scott Kennedy's East Bay Union Railroad. Succulents can rest after soaking up 5-6 hours of direct sun, the minimum for "full sun" plants. Left to right up front live two almost black Swartzkopf aeoniums, Little Ollie dwarf olive tree, a big bunch of sea lettuce and Gollum jade tree.

A National Garden Railway Convention in Las Vegas a few years ago was a great opportunity to collect ideas for realistic miniature deserts. To this New Englander (now gardening in northern California), the railway setting at first looked like a vast arid moonscape. As I looked closer, I saw beautiful gems of silver-blue, coral, and sage-green set in a sea of khaki. Diverse in color and texture, all shared a common goal of conserving moisture.

Here's the skeleton of a desert in progress on the East Bay Union Railroad at one end of a dogbone trackplan. A flagstone plateau supports the track and retains soil while a dry creek provides drainage and a footpath.

Desert Rose volcanic rock is the backbone of Loran and Keith Courpet's Wilco Mine wild west railway.

Why would we northerners want to model the desert? Because we can! It's pretty easy, given the few rules listed below. This chapter is intended to aid railway gardeners who live in both hot and cold climates to model any desert.

Many deserts are located in parks that we can visit in person, online, or in books to get a feel for their characteristics. In western North America alone there are six desert "provinces:" Mohave, Sonoran, Chihuahua, Great Basin, Painted, and Colorado (actually in southern California). Each desert has its own prominent and unique features, as do those in Africa, Australia, and Asia.

Maine to Mohave

There's even a desert in New England! That's right. 11,000 years ago, glaciers deposited a desert-full of sand in Freeport, Maine. Visit *www.desertofmaine.com* to learn about its geological history. Like a huge golf-course sand trap, Maine's "100% certified" desert is surrounded by a forest of pine, spruce, and fir, which would blend nicely into a northern rail line's landscape.

If you'd prefer to model Maine's Sandy River & Rangeley Lakes rather than the Santa Fe, you can legitimately tie in such a desert. It's the perfect excuse for a practical footpath to access other areas of your railway. Instead of blow-away sand, use sifted, compactable decomposed granite in tan-to-pink tones. For easy maintenance, compact the sub layer with drainage material, then mix dry mortar

into the sand. Create slightly peaked dunes, then gently mist. Experiment first, as building materials vary by area.

I prefer a "rainbow of pastels" for a showy desert scene sparkling in the sunniest part of the garden. Typical of the Sonoran and Colorado deserts, giant cacti, like Joshua tree (*Yucca brevifolia*) and saguaro (*Carnegiea gigantea*), can be modeled by succulents found at most garden centers. Some of these are intended for indoors in colder climates, so they will need to be protected or planted in clay pots and brought in during the winter. Outdoors, hide the pots with gravel.

Butte, mesa, dustbowl, flats

These unfamiliar terms define topography that is fascinating and desolate, mysterious yet measurable. As modelers, we need a framework, like a skeleton, to support our models. I use rocks as the backbone to create the structure. Unless you are fortunate to have rock outcroppings on your land, start by visiting several landscape-material yards, as their sources are often different. Ask if they have red, pink, lava, or exotic rock that looks painted. Even if all they have is gray, look for striations of color.

Three shapes of rock will create your skeletal structure: round, flat, and crushed. Half-buried boulders or flagstone against a fence give a mountain-in-the-distance feel. Tumbled flagstone has at least three uses: stacking, leaning for retaining walls, and partially buried (vertically) as a focal point. Crushed or lava rock makes a good

mulch to prevent erosion and cover all soil. I use ginger fines for track ballast.

Because desert plants need excellent drainage, it's imperative to add lots of coarse sand to your planting soil. The best way to ensure drainage is to raise your garden with rock, which will give the plateau/canyon look we associate with this area. Plateaus also serve as roadbed for track, and canyon floors for walking on. Several stand-alone rock formations can be built by stacking combinations of rock with an eye on your picture of the prototype. Now let's flesh out the skeleton.

Succulents to sagebrush

"Fleshy" is just the word to describe the efficient plant group called succulents. It's all about water retention. Cacti belong to this group, with their stems (not leaves) being their canteen. Other xeriphytic (dry loving) plants can be modeled as chaparral-type plants, including sages, lavender, helichrysum, and many Australian and South African plants, newly introduced, with that silvery, waxy look. More and more, you'll find drought-tolerant species in nurseries to save on irrigation.

To drape over cliffs, I like a frost-hardy Australian dwarf *Grevillea* 'Woodburn Pink' with winter-blooming pink flowers here in Zone 9. A similar look is grayish germander (*Teucrium chamaedrys*), frost-hardy to Zone 5. Look in your area for plants with a silver cast to act as a transition to desert: *Artemisia versicolor* 'Sea Foam' is a finely textured, Zone 4 wormwood that lives just as well in Zone 9.

12

Ask the masters

Question: What is your favorite succulent or cactus, or do you have tips for those who want to garden with drought-resistant plants?

Ray Turner
San Jose, California, Zone 9
I like sedums for my desert area. They can survive the summer with little to no water or can thrive and spread with decent watering. There are many varieties. Here are two I have used and like because they look more flower-like. Sedums are fragile—you must take care not to step on them. *Sedum pachyclados* has ½" white flowers. *Sedum kamt* has florets of tiny, ½" long-lasting yellow flowers.

Sedum pachyclados' bluish foliage will get white flowers. *Ray Turner photo*

Sedum kamt in full bloom. *Ray Turner photo*

Sue Jerrems
Las Vegas, Nevada, Zone 10
What grows in the valleys of southern California's low deserts does not apply to the high deserts of Nevada and northern Arizona. I will offer tips for the high desert, which can be translated elsewhere. To make gardening easy, one must choose with care and wear heavy leather gloves!

My favorite relatives of the prickly pear are the teddy bears (*Opuntia bigelovii*), the silver cholla (*O. echinocarpa*) and the tree cholla (*O. imbricata*), also known ominously as the jumping cactus because it attaches with ease to innocent passers-by. All are spreading, with thorns, seemingly innocent-looking but extremely hazardous, yet to me they have such great character with all their fuzzy-looking spikes. Their upright habit provides a unique background.

The hedgehogs (*Echinocereus* sp.) are truly delightful little cacti—low growing and clumping, and most can take a deep freeze. I grow them in more prominent locations because they are typically not too invasive. Flowers range from white, yellow, and pink to orange and deep red. Some bear fruit. Few get taller than a foot. For garden-railroad accent plants, the three best are cotton top (*Echinocactus polycephalus*), strawberry hedgehog (*E. engelmannii*), and Mohave mound (*E. polycephalus* var. *polycephalus*).

Sharon and Bob Yankee
Oregon, Zone 7
We are now on our second garden railway, OHGRR2 (pronounced Ogre 2). At retirement age we realized that we couldn't and shouldn't be moving rocks. Consequently, for our mountains we made use of a clay deposit on our farm. The conifers are doing well in it. However most groundcovers hate it, die out, or grow poorly. We use stonecrop (*Sedum acre*) on the "ridges" to represent the miscellaneous vegetation we see in the

Cascade Range around us. It is happy in the clay soil as well as any other soil. It spreads moderately fast, takes the rainy weather as well as the drought conditions. We are rewarded in summer with bright, golden-yellow flowers that light up our "distant" view. As with all new plantings, water this well until established. Count on us for voting *Sedum acre* as a great drought-resistant plant.

Sue Piper
Southern California, Zone 10
We are developing a ghost town in our railroad that requires an arid, desert-like look. Our two major concerns in the search for suitable plants were that they had to be without thorns or stickers that might injure our dog, who regularly patrols the railway, and they must do well with the over-watering we do to maintain the lush atmosphere of the rest of our line.

Mini Forests by Sky offers three sedum varieties that have a compact, tiny growth. *Sedum stefco* has green and red coloring with very small, white flowers. *S. anglicum* is a lighter green, with blooms varying from white to pink. *S.* 'Blue Carpet' is a beautiful blending of pastel pink, green, and blue. When planted sparsely amid small rocks and surrounded by decomposed granite or gravel, these little succulents provide a lovely springtime-in-the-desert effect.

Sue Piper chose Sedum stefco for its small foliage. *Sue Piper photo*

Don Parker, in his April 2005 *GR* "Miniscaping" column, "Succulents," did an excellent job grouping succulents by genus or type and offering several examples. Then, in December 2007 *GR*, Pat Hayward's "Pathways" column, "Cacti and succulents in the garden railway," showed

us how those who live in Zone 10 find great plants to model the desert. Refer to links in the appendix.

Many a succulent will winter over nicely in Zones 3 and 4 if their feet get good drainage. Northerners will find the chunky rosettes of hen-and-chicks

(*Sempervivum* sp.) in a wide variety of colors and sizes, creating mock barrel cacti and *Agave* sp. Groundcover is covered with the stonecrops (*Sedum* sp.)

You can train twisted junipers, like *Juniperus horizontalis* 'Bar Harbor' (Zone 4-9), into mountainous, wind-blown

Succulents with small leaves and features

Common Name	Botanical Name	Size	Sun/shade	Description, comment	Zones
Tip Top aeonium	Aeonium arborescens 'Tip Top'	18"x18"	sun/pt. sh.	chocolate, green center rosettes on "tree"	9-11
Queen Victoria century plant	Agave victoriae-reginae	4"x6"	sun/pt. sh.	spiny, low dark green rosettes, use caution	9-11
Dwarf aloe	Aloe 'Mini Minnie'	2"x4"	sun	blue-green rosettes, salmon flowers	9-11
Gollum jade tree	Crassula ovata 'Gollum'	18"x24"	sun	smooth tree trunk with green rolled leaves	8-11
Ken Aslet crassula	Crassula sarcocaulis 'Ken Aslet'	18"x24"	sun	smooth tree trunk, tiny leaves, pink flowers	9-11
Hardy African ice plant	Delosperma sp.	6"x24"	sun	low groundcover, bright spring flowers	6-10
Sea lettuce, Sand lettuce	Dudleya caespitosa	3"x3"	sun/pt.sh.	gray-green fleshy rosettes	9-11
Echeveria	Echeveria sp.	6"x6"	sun/pt. sh.	blue-green fleshy rosettes	9-11
Mohave mound hedgehog cactus	Echinocactus polycephalus	18"x24"	sun	spiny mounding cactus	8-11
Firesticks	Euphorbia tirucalli var. rosea	18"x24"	sun	red pencil-like branches form a shrubby tree	9-11
Thimble cactus	Mammillaria fragilis	2"x6"	sun/pt. sh.	white star-like spines cover green "marbles"	9-11
Prickly pear cactus	Opuntia fragilis 'Little Grey Mound'	3"x12"	sun	flat thorny pads are the stems, low mound	3-10
Miniature stonecrop	Sedum requieni, and many others	1"x12"	sun/pt. sh.	green succulent mat, red in fall	3-10
Hen-and-chicks	Sempervivum sp.	2"x6"	sun/pt. sh.	baby rosettes surround central rosette	3-10
Dwarf chalk sticks	Senecio serpens, S.t.mandraliscae	3"x12"	sun/pt. sh.	turquoise-blue fleshy leaves, shrubby	7-10
Dwarf yucca	Yucca nana	12"x12"	sun	white flowers top spiky rosette, white hairs	5-9

Zones are USDA Hardiness Zones

sun/pt. sh. = sun or part shade, sun = at least 5 hours of direct sun per day, size is mature height by width, contingent on exposure and care

specimens of the high desert: prune to maintain a bonsai shape. Restrict their roots with rock slabs a few inches under the surface.

By the way, Bar Harbor juniper grows atop a mountain on Mt. Desert Island in Maine, so named because it is treeless and almost without soil.

Mirage or oasis

I've been finding small sago palms (*Cycas revoluta*) in garden centers. Sagos are like the desert—considered living fossils and among the oldest species on earth. Why not let fossil rocks or petroglyphs tell the story of your oasis? Another small mock palm, *Aeonium arboreum* 'Schwartzkopf', wows us with almost-black leaves in stark contrast to sage-blues.

Watercourses rarely occur in deserts but maybe you'd like to model Painted Desert's falls, plunging from sheer, red canyon cliffs in Zion National Park in Utah. I have visited a model of the Grand Canyon at The Living Desert's garden railway in Palm Desert, California (*www. livingdesert.org*), so I can imagine rafts

floating down a miniature ruddy-red Colorado River.

If you plan to mortar your riverbed liner, use color powders or liquid. If you can't find the buff/red color, there's a simple alternative. Mix a few ounces of ferrous sulfate ($FeSO4$) fertilizer in a quart spray bottle of water and squirt away while the mortar is curing. You'll see green, but the mortar will dry to rust, appropriate for a southwest riverbed.

Details breathe in life—or death

Our first garden railway, built for my young grandson, had to have a small patch of desert. I loved the soft hues and texture; my grandson liked multiplying them by picking off leaves and watching roots grow as they lay on the ground. Then there was the dark side of desert railroading.

The arrow-punctured stagecoach carried hats and baggage but pioneers and horses were mysteriously missing. The watering hole was a buried plastic tray obscured by muddy water, announced by a skull-and-crossbones sign on a Popsicle

stick. Scattered cattle skulls warned skinny Playmobile ponies to go elsewhere but one of them lay stiffly on its side, no longer able to rise. In spite of prominent X's where eyes used to be, the corpse rose from that spot every open house, when sympathetic giants hiked through. Only armadillos and anteaters dared the heat while buzzards waited on dead tree limbs, or was it because they were wired to the tree?

Like a yard sale of costume jewelry, amethyst *Echeveria* rosettes, turquoise chalk sticks, pea-green string of pearls, and coral aloe flowers all spoke the desert language of "come and check us out!" Being in the front of the railway gave a vantage point that secured everyone's attention, drew chuckles, and sometimes blood when someone had to touch that !%@&# cactus.

Reference

Cactus Country: An Illustrated Guide by John A. Murray, Roberts Rinehart Publishers, Boulder, Colorado, 1996

13

Drought-resistant plants and practices to reduce water usage

1. On their M&H Foothill RR, Mike and Holly Crane model Utah's Wasatch Falls (recycled and bio-filtered water) with a down-under transplant, *Grevillea lanigera* 'Coastal Gem' (Zones 9-11), with pink flowers, which will grow sideways to cover much of the rock. Adding color are little apple trees (*Cotoneaster microphylla* 'Emerald Gem', Zones 5-9) in front of a flowering hedge of their California native Manzanita (*Arctostaphylos densiflora* 'Howard McMinn', Zones 6-10).

Are you running the gauntlet between using too much water and watching railroad plants succumb to drying summer heat? Local demonstration gardens prove it's no longer necessary to close your eyes and get summer over with, then repair the damage or pay the water bills. Practicing water conservation can be as simple as choosing xerophytic (dry-loving) plants, as in photo 1.

Planning and design

Xeriscaping is a term, first coined in Denver, Colorado, in 1978, used to define a commitment to water-wise gardening methods, which will help forestall water bans. Succulents are water-thrifty plants but don't always give us the "feel" we want, like the calming, balancing feel of green grass under our feet as we operate trains.

Some water companies now give incentives to replace water-guzzling lawns but fake turf doesn't have the right feel; nor do stones alone, which can be so hot that they cause our air-conditioning bills to rise. A garden that thrives in heat, in suitable, balanced soil, with stone or wood for walkways, walls, and mulch, feels great, especially down the road when it's time to pay the piper.

Efficient irrigation

The first rule of irrigation is to water at the right time of day: in the evening, or overnight and early morning if you run automatic timers. During the day, water simply evaporates instead of feeding the plant. Check your watering's effectiveness by digging to see if the water soaks down to the root zone.

Excessive watering leaches nutrients from roots, depositing them into streams and lakes. If the water runs off, incorporate organic amendment. Terracing to create level ground (see the April 2009 issue of *GR*) also allows irrigation to soak into, not roll off, the surface.

Next, install drip irrigation (photo 2) wherever possible, because sprinklers waste water due to overspray and runoff. A slow rate of watering promotes percolation. Groundcover may be tricky, but low-to-the-ground "drip mist" sprayers suffice—ask for fittings at your hardware store and pick up a product how-to booklet there.

Doesn't it seem that those garden hoses, sprayers, and hose bibbs were designed to leak? To prevent water waste, keep spare rubber washers near your hoses (out of direct sunlight). For no-excuse faucet fixes I install a shut-off (ball) valve between the house and every hose bibb and irrigation-valve assembly. I never have to turn off house water again to fix leaks.

ZEER-uh-fights

Xerophytes don't exactly love zero water; special leaf structure and chemistry adapts

2. After building their Sunset & Boulder Railroad on raised beds, Dennis and Dana Busby demonstrate that it's never too late to install half-inch poly tubing to run drip irrigation across the top of retaining walls disguised as a pipeline. A layer of gravel mulch retains soil moisture and allows water to penetrate to the roots of a xeric, dwarf form of *Myoporum parvifolium* (Zone 8-9). Localized drip irrigation will restrict this somewhat invasive creeper.

3. Robert Smith can't seem to pull up "weed tree" seedlings from under the large, native live oaks (*Quercus agrifolia*) in his yard. Years later, they've evolved into drought-resistant street trees for his large backyard railroad. This one's about 10 years old but will never reach its natural height of 70+ feet, as Robert keeps up with pruning in the bonsai broom style.

Ask the masters

Zones listed are USDA Hardiness Zones

Question: Do you have water-saving plants or horticultural practices that you can recommend?

Frank Lucas
Pleasant Hill, California, Zone 9

We got a little carried away when building our garden railway, and what started out to be a dry stream bed expanded into a full waterfall. Because of our limited real estate, it had to be small, with a small catch pond. The solution was to eliminate the pump, etc. and use a garden-water valve to release new (city) water at the top whenever the trains were running. Since the railway was on an embankment, we used PVC piping to carry the overflow down to our swimming pool to help keep it filled. I guess you could say that we are "double-dipping."

Patience Hoag
Phoenix, Arizona, Zone 10

When we made our waterfall back in 1997, we had a messy, Australian bottle tree smack dab in the middle of our backyard, dropping leaves all over the railway and in the pond. It was a pain. We wanted the shade that the tree offered but, even with drip irrigation, we saw limited success with the plants because of the harsh sun exposure in the areas that were not shaded at all.

When we expanded the railway to include the larger waterfall in 1999-2000, there was no tree in that area of the yard to offer shade, so it made sense

A. A poor start, with roots dependent on frequent, shallow irrigation.

Evaporation

6" soil

Clay subsoil

2nd or 3rd season
- Not much growth
- Roots cannot find water in drought

Figure 1

B. A good start, with deep irrigation followed by dry spells.

Mulch

Soil ball fresh out of nursery pot

12+" soil

- Drainage material & organic matter
- Balanced fertilizer to promote root growth

C.

Tie branch up

Cut

2nd or 3rd season
- Top of plant is allowed to grow big to force root growth down

D. Trimmed to "skinny triangle"

Lateral branch becomes new apex

Remove tie after several weeks

Stout trunk

- Large root system helps to support top growth in times of drought.

Illustration by Marc Horovitz

to put up a large shade cloth to facilitate plant growth. Dan had installed large awnings before and was sure that he could make this idea work, despite the large size. We checked the city building codes first, of course, and found that, because it was not a permanent structure, it was fine. Dan fabricated the frame and the awning company installed the fabric. It is huge and shows little wear in the nearly 10 years it's been up. Along with the shade cloth, we extensively expanded our drip-irrigation system and took greater chances with the types of plants we used.

We enjoyed such success with the plants that first year, that we cut the

bottle tree down and constructed a matching canopy to cover that area. Again, it proved to be well worth the time and cost. In the heat of the summer, I auto-drip every other day for a good 20-30 minutes. Most plants do well with the combination of shade cloth and irrigation—in spite of brutal heat and sun.

Doug Matheson
Ontario, Canada, Zone 4

Here in the Ottawa Valley, we get dependable, adequate rainfall. However, drought-resistant varieties interest me for two reasons: first, I am on sandy soil, which drains almost immediately, and, second, I do most of my garden railroading in heavy shade, where the trees block a good bit of the rain.

Shade-loving plants that withstand drought are fairly rare, but I can recommend the groundcover, periwinkle. It is slow to spread in the shade but, once established, withstands dry, shady conditions well.

For conifers, dwarf hemlock varieties also grow well in shade and withstand drought. Lily-of-the-valley is also tolerant of virtually any shade condition but is very invasive, even with the cold winters here.

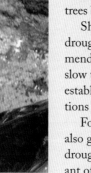

This construction photo shows how Frank Lucas installed a bulkhead fitting on the pond bladder to carry water through a PVC pipe (at the left of his catch basin) to reuse the water elsewhere.

13

In full sun, the pine family does well on dry, sandy soil, although pines are only marginally drought resistant. I like the dwarf mugho pines for my gardens.

I am fortunate in that I can draw water directly from a river for irrigation purposes. This works extremely well with one caveat. Zebra mussels infest most freshwater in the Great Lakes/St. Lawrence basin. I do not have a water feature but, if I did, I would be reluctant to use water from the river for irrigation. The noxious zebra mussel can only be gotten rid of by having a pond freeze to the bottom.

Dick Friedman
Sacramento, California, Zone 9
Most of my railroad is in deep shade from the fruit trees, so heat isn't much of a problem. Finding small plants that can live in shade and clay is the problem. Ray Turner's theory ("treat everything as annuals") has saved my stress level, if not my pocketbook! One perennial, bugleweed, seems to take the heat and not complain, as long as it gets some water.

I have had drip irrigation on my railroad since before it was a railroad! So, I'd say that I am a water saver. During the dryer season (May to October), I water the plants on the railroad about three times a week for about 15-20 minutes, now that all the plants are "mature." From about October to May, I don't water at all, unless the lawn looks stressed. A benefit of using drip (rather than sprinklers) is that only a few weed seeds get watered, so weeding is (somewhat) reduced. Drip is not maintenance free and, in spring, before I return them to automatic, I spend a few minutes checking for blockages and breaks. A few drip nozzles usually are replaced.

Next spring I'm going to look for a dwarf pomegranate. I saw some in Arizona last summer. They look like full-size trees and the fruit is as big as Christmas ornaments. I guess they'll take heat, and I do have some sunny spots on the north side. I'd like to grow one as a living tunnel to hide some return curves.

4. Chip and Sue Gierhart experiment with xerophytes, which thrive among hot rocks in their railway. Not all drought-resistant plants are visibly silver, although their orange-flowered *Helianthemum nummularium* 'Ben Mohr', Zone 5-9) is silvery under its leaves. The 2" trailing verbena (*Verbena* 'Tapiens Blue Violet', Zone 8-11) takes a licking and keeps on ticking, too.

them to drought. Dry-climate plants are far more sensitive to a lack of air in the soil than a shortage of moisture, so good drainage and friable, moderately amended soil is imperative to avoid soggy, rotting feet.

Adding sharp sand to the soil for drainage and planting on raised beds helps, along with minimal fertilizing. To explore Mediterranean-climate gardening, go to *www.dryclimategardening.com.* I also like an informative, online nursery, like *www.highcountrygardens.com*, which features water-thrifty solutions. Then I go to my local nursery to ask about each plant I like.

Native plants have naturally evolved to withstand the rigors of our local climates. Planted in appropriate settings, natives are easy to grow (photo 3). To find a nursery near you selling your area's natives, go to *www.plantnative.org/nd_kytomt.htm.*

Conifers, with their needle-like leaves, and herbs with leathery leaves (photo 4), don't transpire as readily as plants with thin, broad leaves. Silver leaves have either water-conserving waxy coatings or fine hairs. For a low-maintenance lawn in Zones 7-11, learn about St. Augustine grass (*Stenotaphrum secundatum*).

Regardless of plant choice, give all transplants a good start (figure 1), with regular, deep watering, then wean them two or three years later with more

infrequent deep watering. Even non-xeric plants adapt if roots are well developed.

Alternatives
My brother in Massachusetts rarely fights drought; he has saved loads by draining his house gutters all spring into recycled, food-grade drums, then gravity-watering his gardens all summer with free rainwater. See what can be done in Arizona at *www.harvestingrainwater.com.* Anticipating a hot summer, I sometimes spray tender Japanese-maple leaves with an anti-transpirant, Cloud Cover®. A similar product for soil claims to be "crosslinked ampholytic copolymers that are highly absorbent to aqueous electrolyte solutions" or Water Grabber, which holds soil water and slowly releases it to roots.

And mulch more
Mulching conserves soil moisture the way plastic wrap keeps your sandwich fresh. Mulch also reduces weed populations, prevents soil compaction, and keeps soil temperatures more moderate. For miniature gardens, use finer materials. Bagged micro wood chips, sold for orchid-planting medium, is a long-lasting choice and works well under forests. Crushed rock models the desert (photo 2) and wastelands, while smooth pebbles create dry creeks on which to walk so you can reach that uncoupled caboose.

13

Drought-resistant non-succulents

Common Name	Botanical Name	Size	Sun/sh.	Description, comment	Zones
Prickly thrift	*Acantholimon armenum*	8"x15"	sun	spiny subshrub, tiny leaves, tiny flowers	7-9
Mt. Atlas daisy	*Anacyclus pyrethrum* 'Garden Gnome'	4"x8"	sun	ferny leaves, daisy flowers, groundcover	5-9
Kinnikinnick, bearberry	*Arctostaphylos uva-ursi* 'Wood's Compact'	3"x20"	sun/pt.sh	evergreen groundcover, pink spring flowers	2-6
Creeping manzanita	*Arctostaphylos uva-ursi* 'Emerald Carpet'	12"x48"	sh./pt.sh	dark green leathery leaves, woody creeper	6-9
Curlicue sage	*Artemisia versicolor* 'Sea Foam'	8"x18"	sun	silver velvet ferny subshrub, herbaceous	4-10
Dwarf coyote bush	*Baccharis pilularis* 'Twin Peaks'	12"x18"	sun	tiny, oak-like tree, white cottony flowers	7-10
Dwarf weeping bottlebrush	*Callistemon viminalis* 'Little John'	30"x30"	sun	red brushy flowers, tree or hedge	9-11
Little Nicky santolina	*Chamaecyparissus* 'Little Nicky'	12"x15"	sun	gray fluffy subshrub, yellow button flowers	6-9
Small-leaf rockspray	*Cotoneaster microphylla* 'Emerald Gem'	12"x12"	sun/pt.sh	red fruit, look like little apple trees	5-9
Whitlow grass	*Draba sp.* (many low species)	1"x6"	sun	low mounds, alpines in many species	2-9
Silver carpet	*Dymondia margaretae*	6"x6"	sun	gray-green groundcover, yellow flowers	9-11
Thymeleaf buckwheat	*Eriogonum thymoides*	3"x6"	sun	twisted stems, gray leaves, tree-like	3-5
Tiny Tim spurge	*Euphorbia x martinii* 'Tiny Tim'	8"x10"	sun/pt.sh	lime green rosettes, milky poisonous sap	6-9
Woolly grevillea	*Grevillea lanigera* 'Coastal Gem'	12"x36"	sun/pt.sh	pink flowers, sprawling gray-green lshrub	7-11
Rock rose	*Helianthemum nummularium* 'Mutabile Mix'	6"x8"	sun	groundcover, flowers all colors, takes heat	5-9
Juniper	*Juniperus sp.* (See Chapter 21, "Junipers")	2'x12'	sun	scaly leaves, groundcover or shrubby trees	2-11
Dwarf English lavender	*Lavandula angustifolia* 'Nana'	6"x12"	sun	fragrant mounds with lavender flowers	5-10
Sierra Bouquet sage	*Leucophyllum pruinosum* 'Sierra Bouquet'	30"x30"	sun	gray ferny bushy "tree"	8-10
Cotton bush, pearl bluebush	*Maireana sedifolia*	12"x12"	sun/pt.sh	silver-gray tiny leaves on a tree-like bush	9-11
Grape hyacinth	*Muscari, sp.*	12"x6"	sun	bulbs, tubular leaves, grape-like flowers	4-8
Dwarf myoporum	*Myoporum parvifolium* 'Littleleaf Dwarf'	6"x15"	sun	spreading green groundcover, white flowers	8-9
Dwarf myrtle	*Myrtus communis* 'Compacta'	24"x24"	sun/pt.sh	white flowers on shrubby tree	8-10
Little Ollie olive	*Olea sp.* 'Little Ollie'	36"x36"	sun	gray-green oblong leaves, white underneath	10-11
Scented geranium	*Pelargonium crispum* 'French Lace'	24"x24"	sun/pt.sh	crinkly, white edged fragrant leaves	9-11
Dwarf pomegranate	*Punica granatum* 'Nana Emperor'	14"x12"	sun/pt.sh	orange flowers, red fruit	7-11
Dwarf rosemary	*Rosmarinus officinalis* 'Prostratus'	24"x72"	sun	blue flowers, spreads to 8'	7-10
Australian astroturf	*Scleranthus biflorus*	1"x6"	sh./pt.sh	very low almost mossy light green	9-11
Blue-eyed or yellow-eyed grass	*Sisyrinchum sp.*	6"x12"	sun/pt.sh	stiff blades, starry blue or yellow flowers	9-11
Tansy	*Tanacetum haradjani*	6"x12"	sun	blue-gray "ferns," yellow button flowers	7-10
Germander	*Teucrium chamaedrys* or *T. cossoni*	8"x8"	sun/pt.sh	gray-green fuzzy look, blue flowers	5-9
Thyme	*Thymus sp.* (many low varieties)	3"x12"	sun/pt.sh	varieties in red, pink, white flowers	4-9

Size is mature height by width, contingent on care. Sun/pt.sh = sun/part shade exposure. Sun = 5 or more hours of direct sun per day.
Zones are USDA Hardiness Zones

13

Invite critters into your railway

14

Kneeling in the railway garden, I take time to commune with the wildlife passing through. Did you know that whistling makes some butterflies' wings respond defensively to scare off the bird they think is approaching (photos 1, 2)? It was a typical gardener who discovered this tidbit by paying attention. One day I met, face-to-face, a seemingly fearless ruby-crowned kinglet. I thought I was one with the universe until I read that kinglets are friendly with any human who happens to be hanging out under shrubbery. Enjoying "your" railway critters, wild or tame, is the topic of this chapter.

1. We're looking at the folded wing of a Painted Lady butterfly, looking back at us with faux eyes to scare away a predator (the photographer). Butterfly-bush tubular flowers provide nectar.

2. The same Painted Lady butterfly spreads its wings, perhaps to visit Dan and Joyce Pierce's many flowering host plants in their train gardens.

3. When Bob Vidal feeds his fish, he runs his orange Railking hopper car onto a specially wired section of track that comes with the car (upper track). Pushing a button tips the hopper and out pours fish food to delight his visitors, as well as the fish. Japanese maple trees shade the pond in summer, cooling the water, which mirrors greenery, bridges, and trains for an alternate view of the railway.

4. Paul Gamlin's "Beatrix Potter Train" crosses one of many beautiful bridges on Richard and Melinda Murray's Green Hills Railroad.

5. Irene and Bob Brown make water troughs for birds, not cattle. Sprinkler water fills the trough, which is lined with a plastic tray normally sold for kitchen utensils.

6. The author enjoys watching the Anna's hummingbird enjoying water. Running shallow water over a flat flagstone is a sure way to attract short-legged birds and dragonflies, if the territorial hummer will allow visitors to his shower. The cutleaf Japanese maples like a little bath, too.

Some ask, "Why? Isn't it enough to deal with weather, mechanical, and civil-engineering issues?" That was my response until other railroad gardeners inspired me with their success. The connection they joyfully created with nature inspired me to also share that joy, and still run trains!

Why drive to some remote park to lower my blood pressure when I can just open the door to the backyard? Watching nature in action is a proven therapy that allows us to justify our hobby: "Honey, Doc says I have nature-deficit disorder and need a 'green prescription.'" (*http://en.wikipdia.org/wiki/Green_prescription*)

Water!

You'll find many books and online resources on how to attract wildlife but "water" tops the list. Many of us have created wonderful water features for our railways to model a scene and, of course, to provide us with something to install

Miniatures that attract fun critters

Common Name	Botanical Name	Size	Sun/sh.	Description, comment	Critters	Zones
Japanese maple	*Acer palmatum* var.	4'x4'	sun/pt.sh.	single-stemmed small tree, palmate leaves	hummer	5-8
Pearly everlasting	*Anaphalis margaritacea*	36"x24"	sun/pt.sh.	woolly-gray foliage, white globular flowers	butterfly	3-8
Creeping manzanita	*Arctostaphylos uva-ursi* 'Emerald Carpet'	18"x72"	sh./pt.sh.	dark green leathery leaves, woody creeper	birds	6-9
Dwarf butterfly bush	*Buddleia* 'Blue Chip'	18"x18"	sun	blue flowers all summer, woody subshrub	butterfly	6-9
Nanho Blue butterfly bush	*Buddleia davidii* 'Nanho Blue'	5'x5'	sun	small woody shrub, blue flowers	butterfly	5-10
Scotch heather	*Calluna vulgaris* 'Robert Chapman'	18"x18"	sun/pt.sh.	evergreen shrubby	birds, b-fly	4-6
California wild lilac	*Ceanothus* 'Centennial'	6'x7'	sun	sprawler, deep blue pom pom flowers	hum'r, b-fly	9-11
Dwarf spurge laurel	*Daphne* 'Lawrence Crocker'	6'x24"	sun	fragrant mauve flowers, leathery leaves	hum'r, b-fly	4-9
Thyme-leaf fuchsia	*Fuchsia thymifolia, F. microphylla*	12"x12"	sh./pt.sh.	red, pink, white flowers	hummer	10-11
Dwarf English lavender	*Lavandula angustifolia* 'Nana'	6"x12"	sun	fragrant grayish leaves, purple flowers	bees, b-fly	5-1-
Statice	*Limonium sinuatum*	12"x12"	sun	many colors of flowers on winged stems	bees, b-fly	na
Rosemary	*Rosmarinus officinalis* 'Prostratus'	24"x24"	sun	evergreen, fragrant foliage, blue flowers	bees, b-fly	8-10
Japanese spirea	*Spirea nipponica* 'Little Princess'	24"x24"	sun	deciduous shrub, deep pink flowers	butterfy	4-8
Korean lilac	*Syringa meyeri* 'Palibin', S.m.'Miss Kim'	60"x72"	sun	small hedge, pale pink fragrant flowers	hum'r, b-fly	3-7
Thyme	*Thymus* sp.	4"x10"	sun	fragrant mat, pink, white, red flowers	bees, b-fly	4-9
Red clover	*Trifolium pratense*	6"x 8"	sun/pt.sh.	mat, red flowers appease woodchucks	bees, wdchk	3-9
Tapiens Blue verbena	*Verbena* 'Tapiens Blue'	6"x15"	sun	groundcover, purple flowers	butterfly	8-11

Size is mature height by width (contingent on care, climate, etc.) after several seasons. Width dimensions are intended to show relative spread.

Sun/sh = sun or shade orientation; pt.sh. = partial shade orientation, etc. Critters: hum'r and hummer = hummingbird, b-fly = butterfly, wdchk = woodchuck

Zones are USDA Hardiness Zones, na = non-hardy annual

bridges over. All sorts of critters, with any number of legs, wings, and fins, want water, and they do find it. Have you ever seen bees or butterflies sucking water from mud or wet rocks? Pet fish need care but why not make it fun, like Bob Vidal does at feeding time, with a spring-loaded hopper car that dispenses fish pellets with the push of a remote button (photo 3)?

How to raise fish in a pond could be a book in itself but your local expert can help you avoid survival-of-the-fittest

backyard battles. Richard and Melinda Murray went to a local pond-and-fish expert, then installed all the necessary equipment behind their mountainside water feature to keep their koi healthy and their pond clean. Their pond is central to their railway and afforded Richard a reason to build an exquisite wooden bridge on realistic stone abutments (photo 4). Steep embankments and deep water prevent those masked bandits (raccoons) from fishing out the pets.

Ask the masters

Zones listed are USDA Hardiness Zones

Question: How have you hosted wildlife or pets to share your railway?

Doug Matheson
Ontario, Canada, Zone 4

In our rural railway garden, it is not a question of inviting critters into the railroad garden but more a question of living amiably with them, as they *will* come. I do not like to pointlessly kill or harm any wildlife and we enjoy seeing what nature offers us.

The first step is to build a railroad that is somewhat critter proof. By elevating the trackage, which is more comfortable to work on anyway, I have found that the outer perimeter of raised track reliably discourages foraging deer from entering the railway. Next, I limit my buildings to just a very few, solidly built structures to discourage insects and, especially, squirrels and chipmunks, from taking up residence. I have come to enjoy the antics of the hordes of squirrels roaming the garden and removing any small detail they can find.

Although a few songbirds come to our shady garden, we mostly see northern birds like cardinals and jays. I encourage them with birdhouses and nearby feeders, as watching birds is a joy. Generally, I have had few problems with my plantings. The odd plant browsed by a rabbit or other critter is just regarded as the "cost of doing business." While I would prefer not to host certain critters, the vast majority are interesting to watch and reasonably easy to accommodate.

Cecil Easterday
Chicago area, Zone 5

Inviting wildlife into the garden is part of what makes gardening and the garden railroad fun! Our coal tipple has housed a nest of Carolina wrens for the past three years, the cardinals nest in the viburnum bushes, and the cedar waxwings love the berries on the amelanchier! In the winter, birds roost in a pile of branches we leave in the woods for that

purpose. Honeysuckle feeds vines to deer and nectar to hummingbirds, which also love our bee balm. Coneflower seed feeds the goldfinches.

We discovered a host plant for the American Lady butterfly caterpillar in *Antennaria dioica* (pussytoes, Zone 3-9, see "Plant portraits," *GR*, October 2003). It is great for a sunny, hot, and dry area in clay soil. In early June, the caterpillar devastates the plant foliage. Then in July (if the birds don't get the caterpillars first) there are dozens of these gorgeous critters flitting around the yard. It does leave a hole in the garden until August, when the plant starts coming back, but it is well worth it!

This spring, a doe left her tiny fawn in an area covered with bishop's weed (*Aegopodium podagraria* 'Variegatum'). The little one settled under the leaves until barely visible. Sometime during the night the doe came back and moved her fawn. Living in a deeply wooded area, we have discovered that it is much more fun to live with the wildlife (deer included) than try to fight them. [See Cecil's article about regulating her deer in *GR*, December 2003.]

Bill Hewitt
Mansfield, Massachusetts, Zone 5

We have a family of garter snakes that live in our railway. They like to lie on the track for warmth. Here, (right) one of the snakes looks like something out of a Japanese monster movie.

Dick Friedman
Sacramento, California, Zone 9

I've got a bunch of wild and domestic critters on my railroad. Squirrels love my apples and birds drop in for a drink from the pond, home to goldfish and mosquito fish—at least until they reach "snackin' size" for the raccoons. I used to buy big, fancy goldfish—shubunkins, I think they're called—but they disappeared too quickly; so now I only buy "feeder fish" and give them a few months of life. It's fun to watch them grow. This year, I put plants in the pond, which now cover much of the surface. Maybe the raccoon won't notice .…

Cecil Easterday's daughter found this black swallowtail butterfly sipping from tall verbena. Queen Anne's lace is usually the host plant for the black swallowtail caterpillar. *Cecil Easterday photo*

Bill and Liana Hewitt are hosting a Japanese film crew to shoot the monster movie "Snakezilla" in their Southpark & Dogbark Railroad. *Anna Kincheloe photo*

Frank Lucas
Pleasant Hill, California, Zone 9
Sometimes our railroad operates as a "feeder line." When not running, the freight train is parked on the north loop with peanuts in the gondolas. The picture (right) says it all.

Sue Piper
Lakeside, California, Zone 10
Our miniature Schnauzer, Jasmine, has taken over as guardian and chief patrol officer. First thing in the morning, last thing in the evening, and at periodic times during the day, she follows her self-appointed route along the track, crosses the stone bridge, and stops at the runway to look back at the house to see if anyone is having a snack, then continues to the far end. She stands on the track watching oncoming trains and steps off just in time, plays red-light-green-light with lizards on the back wall, discourages birds from landing to eat the "apples" on my cotoneasters, and wakes us up at night when a 'possum or raccoon is on the back fence, threatening to come down into her railroad.

We have made some minor concessions. We insert a brass wire into a leg of our figures to stick in the ground so they remain standing. We do not plant the brittle Hokkaido elms adjacent to her typical routes. In return, when we are busy working in the railroad, she brings over a toy or two and carefully places them, then stands back waiting for us to notice her contribution. We have been very fortunate!

Bob and Sky Yankee
Mulino, Oregon, Zone 7
Our first garden railway (*GR*, February 1995) had two streams and a pond. To our delight, many wild birds claimed the territory. Sparrows bathed in the North Branch and preened on a nearby bridge. Goldfinches claimed the South Branch and preened on trees edging the pond. Another bonus was our first experience with a dragonfly. A rather large one claimed the shallow waters of the pond, aggressively defending its territory by dive-bombing us as we walked by. If we sat quietly, we were allowed to stay and watch its raid on bugs. Our current railway has no water feature but still attracts

At Frank and Donna Lucas's Chug Railway, a scrub jay picks up lunch "to go" on his way home. *Sue Piper photo*

Jasmine the watchdog guards the Pipers' Serusso Springs Railway when not decorating it with her toys. *Bill Hewitt photo*

the birds. Early spring brings a "bull" robin, as Bob calls it, that claims the trees at High Camp. When he moves on to help rear his young, a song sparrow moves in. Both species give us beautiful songs and much entertainment. The saying, "If you build it, they will come," has worked for us.

7. Leaving the dead top on this bald cypress tree allows the dragonfly to look out for predators, like birds, which frequently bathe on the "steps" covered with shallow, falling water. In the spring, frogs hide between rocks and bellow their nighttime serenade.

9. Jerry and Alison Ogden's cat patrols their Possom Creek Railroad.

8. On the Browns' Tuolumne County Narrow Gauge Railroad, resident lepidopterist, Irene, encourages her favorite butterflies by planting food plants for all stages of growth. Knowing where the host plants grow told her that this Variable Checkerspot butterfly larva had to crawl quite a distance to pupate on their girder bridge. It's practically a pet!

Wild animals are sometimes challenged to find enough water, so we gardeners can help them out (photo 5). Shallow depth is critical to allow short-legged birds to bathe and safely drink. I've built several water features with water flowing over a large, flat stone, specifically to allow birds to alight there.

Our driven hummer

A daily ritual of our resident hummingbird held me in a trance every time I witnessed his bathing style (photo 6). First, it hovered over the waterfall's top, flat stone, looking in all directions. Then he zipped over to the wire fence 10 feet away, where he perched like a sentinel. At least three more times he went over to the waterfall, hovering inches from his bath water, head snapping back and forth. Finally he plopped onto the wet flat rock, pressed his wings out and allowed water to rush around his outstretched body. In just a few seconds he shot for the wire fence and preened his feathers, occasionally leaping up to shake off bath water like a shaggy dog.

Thyme-leaf fuchsia (*Fuchsia thymifolia*, Zones 8-11) provided many snacks for that hummingbird. Use the keyword

"hummingbird" to search for nectar plants at *www.highcountrygardens.com.*

Habitat

Most gardeners will be relieved to know that leaving those unraked, leafy sections of the yard provides nesting sites for birds and butterflies (photo 7). Native plants are the best source of food and shelter for these beautiful flying creatures. If you want to attract certain species, you can look up what to grow for food plants (photo 8). Look for compact plants, like rabbit- and deer-resistant dwarf lavender (*Lavandula angustifolia* 'Nana', Zone 5-10) and dwarf butterfly bush (*Buddleia davidii* 'Nanho Blue', Zone 5-10). "Nana" means small. A guide for butterfly host plants is listed at the end of this nursery web page: *www.arrowheadalpines.com/ arrowhead_alpines_2008_catalog.pdf.*

Some caveats: Plant the rangier plants farther from track and buildings. Use a diversity of plant material. Turn off track power ASAP to prevent little guys from committing suicide. Avoid pesticides, which kill the beauties along with the beasts. And be sure to provide yourself with seating areas scattered about so you can watch unaware (photo 9).

Isolate your garden from nuisance nibblers

15

You discover the animal kingdom has invaded your railway empire. A call to arms! Your first strategy may be to respond with weapons of mass destruction. Steering clear of the melee, let's look at armor instead of arms, information instead of incendiaries. After all, we need to get down in the trenches, in close contact with our plants, whether pruning, adjusting rail joiners, or re-railing train wheels.

Bill Hewitt's Dogbark and Southpark Railroad needed protection from his curious and dig-crazy dogs. In front of each section of his ground-level layout he planted a thorny hedge of barberry (*Berberis thunbergii* 'Atropurpurea', Zones 4-8). This is a dog's view of the garden.

Dwarf silver sword (*Yucca nana*) certainly will keep critters away, but it might put you away, too. Succulent sempervivums surround the spikes.

On Duane and Margi Hyer's Ivy Hill & Gopherton Railroad, these two (three?) fellows are armed with curiosity, probably the best way to deal with small rodent holes.

Botanic gardens are good places to learn about deer-resistant plants brought in from other countries. Here's a Turkish tansy growing in Zone 5, Denver, Colorado.

No longer will raccoons bed down in this tunnel and knock over trains. Two rudimentary posts hold the wire mesh door in place.

After skunks made a home in this tunnel, the author built a permanent hinged and latched door for this portal. Not prototypical, but practical.

Some inorganic pesticides can backfire and cause an unhealthy environment or "friendly fire" for fragile seniors and children. Listening to others' successes, I've listed some kinder, gentler organic solutions for prevention—from derivatives of the chrysanthemum plant to mechanical devices and finally a list of mini-plants known to repel critters. Sometimes the worst pests are those we invite into our homes!

Dogs and cats (maybe)

Some miniature plants get prickly and are aptly named for their barbs, like barberry, which makes an effective barrier for dogs, if surrounding your garden. Cats don't like to walk on barberry or rose trimmings scattered

underneath, so one barrier works for both pets.

When Gary Robinson built his raised bed layout, his tall poodle thought it was great fun to jump up onto the garden ... up and down, up and down, because she could. Having taught her to stay off the furniture, Gary trained the dog by commanding, "Off the bed, Ginger!" And it worked.

Give pets their rightful places in the yard: their business areas, resting rooms in shade and sun, and dog runs to patrol the grounds. Of course cats are a little more independent and will likely find a way into the garden when nature calls. Pet stores sell sprays to keep cats off furniture, but they will probably wash away quickly outdoors. Gluing the

top inch of track ballast with Quikrete® Concrete Bonding Adhesive (1:3 with water) prevents cats from scratching away the soft dry gravel.

Gophers, moles, and voles

To protect her full-scale garden from gophers, my sister has to put every plant into chicken-wire baskets before transplanting them into her yard. Otherwise the burrowing beasts eat the roots and then pull the tops down under for dessert. Regional gardening reporter, Sue Piper, lined whole beds with wire mesh to accommodate the mini-gardening style of planting very small plants close together. Gophers make a huge mess when they burrow, but moles and voles, not so much. Plug-

Scare off critters with a horrible looking dino. A motion sensor triggers a ferocious sounding roar, powered by batteries.

German statice could easily portray cherry trees in full spring bloom. Scratchy "everlasting" flowers repel animals.

Dwarf Japanese spirea doesn't offer any visible signs that it's deer resistant, but it's been observed to resist browsing.

Margi and Duane Hyer heard that deer will often graze near cattle because they feel protected. Maybe they're after the cows' salt block too. The field is Australian astroturf on the IH&GRR.

Daffodils and other members of the lily family taste too spicy for deer and rabbits. *Joan Scheiwiller photo*

ging their holes or sprinkling them with cayenne pepper may deter them and cause them to go elsewhere, but if not, be thankful you don't have gophers. Hanging soap bars made from animal fat near entrance holes scares off some rodents, too.

Raccoons, skunks, woodchucks, rats

Most rodents have evolved to be stealthy nocturnal prowlers. One of my most unpleasant tasks was to evict a rather civilized raccoon from homesteading a long tunnel. For weeks while the train operator was busy on other things, Mr. Raccoon used one tunnel end for his daytime bedroom and the other end (where the trains were housed overnight) for his bathroom.

See the photo for our solution. Actually that wasn't as bad as the worry of evicting a skunk from a tunnel. See the photo for our solution to that problem.

If raccoons and skunks are problems in the daytime, it's nothing compared to their nighttime eating habits. They enjoy rolling back groundcovers looking for juicy grubs and protein-rich earthworms. One family was able to rid their dug-up yard of raccoons with humane Havahart® traps, but check local laws, as it may be illegal to "relocate" them. Check out www.havahart.com/store/animal-repellents for repellents in spray bottles. Electronic devices sold at garden centers emit a frequency that keeps raccoons, skunks and deer away. Woodchucks prefer foot-high red

clover (*Trifolium pratense*, Zones 3-8) to cultivated garden plants, so plant a little patch to appease them. If they don't eat it, you can make a red-clover tonic tea.

Unfortunately, many of us have quit feeding birds to eliminate an excess of rats and squirrels, which feast on birdfeed spillage. They have become an urban nightmare. I believe it's better to try to catch and recycle spillage and keep attracting the birds that also eat the insects in my garden.

Deer and rabbits

Fond memories of Bambi and Peter Rabbit soften hearts at the bucolic sight of young deer and bunnies … at first! Then after planting $200-worth of miniature plants we're ready to get out

Pest-deterrent miniatures*

Common Name	Botanical name	Size	Sun/shade	Description, comment	Zones
Annuals and biennials rarely eaten					
Floss flower	*Ageratum houstonianum* 'Blue Danube'	8"x8"	sun	fuzzy blue mounds on 2" leaves	annual
Polka-dot plant	*Hypoestes phyllostachya*	12"x12"	pt. shade	pink dots on 3"-long leaves, moist soil	10-11
Edging lobelia	*Lobelia erinus* 'Riviera Mix'	6"x10"	sun/pt.sh.	blue, lavender, pink or white flowers	9-11
Forget-me-not	*Myosotis sylvatica* 'Victoria Blue Dwarf'	10"x12"	pt. shade	light blue tiny flowers, biennial	3-8
Sweet basil	*Ocimum basilicum* 'Basilico Greco'	8"x8"	sun	compact plants, small spicy, edible leaves	annual
Parsley	*Petroselinum crispum*	8"x8"	sun/pt.sh.	curly edible foliage, biennial	7-9
French marigold	*Tagetes patula*	8"x8"	sun	fragrant yellow, orange, red flowers	annual
Verbena	*Verbena* x 'Tapiens Blue'	2"x12"	sun	rambling serrated leaves, purple clusters	7-10
Perennials rarely eaten					
Dwarf yarrow, sneezeweed	*Achillea tomentosa* 'King Edward'	6"x12"	sun	gray-green lacy leaves, yellow buttons	3-10
Chocolate chip bugleweed	*Ajuga reptans* 'Valfredda' syn. 'Choc.Chip'	4"x10"	sun/pt.sh.	chocolate tinged strap leaves, blue flowers	4-9
Chives	*Allium schoenoprasum*	10"x12"	sun	oniony hollow stems, pink puffballs	2-9
Garlic chives	*Allium tuberosum*	12"x6"	sun	white flowers, hollow oniony leaves	4-8
Silver mound	*Artemisia schmidtiana*	12"x18"	sun	silver feather dusters in a mound	4-8
Basket of gold	*Aurinia saxatilis* 'Compacta'	12"x18"	sun	blue-gray foliage, gold tufts	3-7
Alpine hard fern	*Blechnum penna-marina*	3"x 6"	sh./pt.sh.	true fern, leathery dark fronds, moist soil	5-10
Lily-of-the-valley	*Convallaria majallis*	8"x10"	sh./pt.sh.	bulb plant with ¼" white bells on spikes	4-7
Rock brake fern	*Cryptogramma crispa*	8"x10"	sh./pt.sh.	true fern, parsley-like fronds	2-8
Clove pinks	*Dianthus* 'White Mound'	4"x8"	sun/pt.sh.	blue-green grassy mounds, starry flowers	3-9
Fringed bleeding heart	*Dicentra* 'King of Hearts'	8"x 12"	sun/shade	heart flowers, poisonous plant parts	3-8
Barrenwort	*Epimedium grandiflorum* 'Saturn'	6"x12"	shade	fine-toothed 2" leaves, white starry flowers	4-8
Dwarf Martin's spurge	*Euphorbia* x *martinii* 'Tiny Tim'	6"x12"	sun/pt.sh.	pinwheel leaves, chartreuse flowers	6-9
Sweet woodruff	*Galium odoratum* syn. *Asperula oderata*	8"x 12"	sun/shade	whorled leaves on 4-6" stems, moist soil	4-8
German statice	*Goniolimon tataricum* 'Woodcreek'	12"x12"	sun	fine white flowers cover large basal leaves	4-9
Creeping baby's breath	*Gypsophila repens* 'Rosea'	6"x12"	sun/pt.sh.	airy plant suspends tiny rosy flowers	3-9
Dwarf candytuft	*Iberis sempervirens* 'Little Gem'	4"x10"	sun/pt.sh.	evergreen mat, bright white spring flowers	4-9
Deadnettle	*Lamium galeobdolon*	10"x12"	pt. shade	larger silver/green leaves, yellow flowers	4-9
Dwarf English lavender	*Lavandula angustifolia* 'Nana'	6"x10"	sun/pt.sh.	fragrant mounds, lavender spiky clusters	5-10
Perennial blue flax	*Linum perenne*	12"x6"	sun	true blue flowers on spindly stems	4-9
Water forget-me-not	*Myosotis scorpioides*	10"x12"	sun	tiny blue or white flowers, moist soil	3-8
Dwarf daffodil	*Narcissus* 'Tete a Tete'	10"x10"	sun	yellow cup and saucers, strap leaves, bulbs	4-11
Catnip, catmint	*Nepeta* x *faassenii* 'Walker's Low'	18"x18"	sun/pt.sh.	tall lavender clusters, moist soil	3-8
Dwarf oregano	*Origanum vulgare* 'Nanum'	6"x10"	sun/pt.sh.	edible, compact plants, pink flowers	4-9
Allegheny spurge	*Pachysandra procumbens*	8"x12"	sun/shade	fluffly groundcover, whorled green leaves	4-9
Japanese pachysandra	*Pachysandra terminalis*	8"x12"	sun/shade	fluffly groundcover, whorled green leaves	4-9
Spring cinquefoil	*Potentilla neumanniana* 'Nana'	2"x6"	sun/pt.sh.	toothed leaflets, yellow flowers	3-9
Alpine cinquefoil	*Potentilla villosa*	2"x6"	sun	white edged leaflets, yellow flowers	3-5
Prostrate rosemary	*Rosmarinus officinalis* 'Prostratus', 'Irene'	12"x8'	sun/pt.sh.	edible needle-like leaves, blue flowers	9-11
Sinaloa sage	*Salvia sinaloensis*	6"x10"	sun/pt.sh.	blue flowers, annual in some zones	8-11
Siberian squill	*Scilla siberica*	4"x8"	sun/pt.sh.	bulb with grassy leaves, blue flowers	4-8
Little Princess dwarf spirea	*Spiraea nipponica* 'Little Princess'	2'x3'	sun	dense mound, pink flowers, deciduous	3-9

15

Common Name	Botanical name	Size	Sun/shade	Description, comment	Zones
Dwarf tansy	Tanacetum haradjani	6"x12"	sun	blue-gray "ferns," yellow button flowers	7-10
Thyme, all species and cultivars	Thymus sp.	2-12"x1'	sun/pt.sh.	all thymes resist nibblers, mats or airy bush	3-9
Whitley's speedwell	Veronica whitleyi	4"x8"	sun/pt.sh.	dull green mat, blue flowers	4-8
Labrador violet	Viola labradorica	3"x6"	pt. shade	purplish green heart leaves, purple flowers	3-9
Dwarf silver sword	Yucca nana	12"x12"	sun	blue spiky succulent rosette	5-9
Trees and shrubs rarely eaten					
Shaina Japanese maple	Acer palmatum 'Shaina'	4'x4'	sun/pt.sh.	easily pruned shorter, tree-like, red leaves	5-8
Dwarf coyote bush	Baccharis pilularis 'Twin Peaks'	12"x18"	sun	shrub, prune to look like an oak tree	7-10
Crimson pygmy dwarf barberry	Berberis thunbergii 'Atropurpurea Nana'	18"x18"	sun/pt.sh.	barbed shrub, red/green leaves	4-8
Trost's dwarf birch	Betula pendula 'Trost's Dwarf'	3'x 2'	sun/pt.sh.	weeping willow look, easy to keep low	3-9
Butterflybush	Buddleja davidii 'Blue Chip'	15"x18"	sun	shrub with long blue clusters	5-9
Green Gem dwarf boxwood	Buxus x 'Green Gem'	2'x2'	sun/pt.sh.	small evergreen, hedge or shrubby tree	5-9
Foya Scotch heather	Calluna vulgaris 'Foya'	10"x15"	sun	scale-like red foliage, moist acidic soil	4-7
Compact threadleaf falsecypress	Chamaecyparis pisifera 'Filifera Nana'	4'x4'	sun/pt.sh.	find golden evergreen shrub, trim for tree	4-8
Spring heath	Erica carnea	10"x10"	sun	needle leaves, spring flowers	5-7
Finetooth holly	Ilex serrata 'Koshobai'	12"x12"	sun/pt.sh.	white flowers, red fruit, moist soil	5-9
Dwarf Japanese garden juniper	Juniperus procumbens 'Nana'	12"x3'	sun/pt.sh.	blue-green, easy, creeping	4-9
Dwarf heavenly bamboo	Nandina domestica 'Wood's Dwarf'	18"x18"	sun/pt.sh.	dense, compact growth, red fall color	6-9
Dwarf Norway spruce	Picea abies 'Pumila'	3'x3'	sun	globe shape can be pruned to tree	3-8
Dwarf Alberta spruce	Picea glauca 'Conica'	4'x3'	sun/pt.sh.	cone-shaped conifer for forests, prune often	4-8
Dwarf Colorado blue spruce	Picea pungens 'Montgomery'	18"x24"	sun	blue globe conifer, prune to shape	3-8
Mountain lily, andromeda	Pieris japonica 'Little Heath'	2'x2'	sun/pt.sh.	white spring flowers, small leaves red in fall	5-8
Dwarf mugo pine	Pinus mugo 'Donna's Mini'	10"x12"	sun	dense round mound, like a sea urchin	2-9
Dwarf mugo pine	Pinus mugo 'Mops'	10"x12"	sun	dense round mound, like a sea urchin	2-9
Beauvronensis Scots pine	Pinus sylvestris 'Beauvronensis'	2'x3'	sun	dense mound of tight branching	5-8

* Please note this list is not complete and success is varied. Plants with the same genus name are usually also pest deterrents.

Handle all plants with gloves as some may be irritants. Unless specified as edible, consider plants to be poisonous and do not eat any parts of plants.

Size is mature height by width in ten years, contingent on care. Sun is five or more hours direct sun/day. Sun/pt.sh. = sun or partial shade.

Zones are USDA Hardiness Zones

15

the big guns. If only Farmer Mac-Gregor had the internet!

Products and advice are available at *www.highcountrygardens.com*. Staff there suggest using three of their stinky deer sprays in random succession to confuse the deer and rabbits. Rocking water fountains that make a clocking sound and automatic electronic-sound makers are two ways to scare them off, but the critters eventually figure out our ploy, just as the motion-sensor sprinklers work only for a short time. The best bet for deterring deer and rabbits is to alternate all the guns in your arsenal. Variety is the spice. Two such deer repellents are Plant Pro-Tecs® (garlic)

Units, deer repellent clips, and Liquid Fence® (urine) spray.

See chart of "Pest-deterrent miniatures." You'll still need to protect newly planted deer-resistant plants, but only in the spring and early summer when deer are young and trying everything. If stinky sprays become too unpleasant and you decide to build a fence, make it high and solid. When deer can't see the opposite side, they won't jump.

Why do deer avoid our neighbor's plants, but go after our same-species plants, fresh from the nursery? Nurseries use nitrate-phosphate-potash-based fertilizers to grow plants as quickly as possible. Remember from Chapter 7

Deer-rabbit-rodent-repellent recipe

Two eggs, garlic cloves, cayenne pepper, castor oil (helps adhere the mix to plants up to 30 days)

Blend all with some water in the kitchen blender and wait two days to "ripen" the brew. Strain into a spray bottle and add more water. Spray on plants known to be favorite food for your pests and new nursery plants. Deer don't like their food associated with dead animals, like eggs and soap.

Spruce are deer resistant. Spraying this dwarf Colorado blue spruce (*Picea pungens* 'Saint Mary's Broom', Zones 3-9) with horticultural oil would mask its lovely blue cast.

Green Japanese spurge repels critters, which don't like spurge's milky sap. Best of all, it's maintenance free.

White sweet woodruff and baby blue forget-me-nots bloom in spring and cover the ground while resisting deer and rabbits.

A snail waits in hiding for the host's train party to finish so he can begin his nocturnal nibbling.

Pungent silver thyme (*Thymus* sp. 'Argenteus', Zones 4-10) borders the garden like a sentry to ward off predators attacking its companion plants within the fenced little city.

that we discussed how inorganic fertilizers are made from salts? Well, deer love salt as much as cows like their salt blocks. Nursery plants are as irresistible as popcorn. As soon as you plant, protect them with some of the above methods and wean them from the salts. Feed roots with compost, organic seaweed solution, and rock phosphate or bone meal, sparingly. Sprinkle hardwood ashes sparingly for potassium around plants. Give your plants amended soil then starve your little guys a bit—make them dig down for nutrients.

Winged wonderbeasts

Some of the most beautiful birds are the elegant egrets and great blue herons. Long legs allow them access to shallow backyard ponds where they gobble up fancy foot-long fish and barely make it off the ground to fly home. See the photo for one gardeners' revenge. Another group of winged bandits are the jays who like to line their nests with 3" figures ($5 each), presumably to entertain the kids while they're out shopping for peanuts. Prop up your people with wire nails glued into legs and anchor them into the ground.

Bugs!

Chapter 7, "Mini-plant care," mentions spraying sucking insects, like aphids, with a natural insecticidal-soap spray (Safer®, for example). You can make your own with one teaspoon of dish

detergent mixed with one quart of water in a spray bottle. Spice it up with ground, strained garlic and cayenne pepper or hot sauce, but don't let the wind spray it in your eyes—ouch! Reapply after soaking rains. Safer® Bio Neem is a plant-derived, natural insecticide and repellent that controls over 30 common insect pests.

Sometimes all you need is a sharp stream of hose water to loosen bugs, especially spider mites, but if your trees have densely packed branches the water won't get in there and dead leaves provide a safe nest for bugs. Snails and slugs will die crawling over a sprinkling of razor sharp (to them) iron phosphate Sluggo®, but it's safe for pets. Bonsai sensei (teachers) recommend spray-

Nine-inch-high barrenwort tolerates deep shade, drought, competition from roots, and deer better than most plants. Thick leathery leaves are this plant's defense.

These ants filing up and down the thymeleaf fuchsia stems (*Fuchsia thymifolia*, Zones 8-11) are "milking a herd" of aphids. Soap sprays get rid of both insects.

Amazingly, no harm was done when Canadian Elizabeth Claridge found a bear and two cubs sniffing bearberry (*Archtostaphylos uva ursi* 'Wood's Compact', Zones 2-8).

Maybe this crop of strong-smelling marigolds will be interspersed in the garden as companion plants for color and bug control.

To protect his fish from pilfering long legged birds, Brian Wenn mounted a scary alligator in his pond then draped netting over a few black towers, which barely obscure the water scene.

ing conifers and deciduous broadleaf shrubs during the wintertime with a horticultural oil (Volck®, for example) to smother insects, eggs and larvae, which are dormant and over-wintering on bark and leaves. The only problem with this treatment is that the oil can mask the blue "bloom" on some conifers darkening the powdery gray-blue color we bought them for. Conifers with the waxy blue bloom are usually resistant to pests so avoid spraying them with oil. Other than that issue, "dormant oil" spray is a great prophylactic.

When the going gets tough, the tough gardener gets going to the garden center for more powerful weapons. Fortunately, natural insecticides made from chrysanthemum are much safer to use than some inorganic pesticides, some of which have been banned. Permethrin is a human-made version of the long used natural pyrethrins found in African daisy. It's safe enough, according to the EPA, to use in human apparel (Sloggers® Garden Outfitters) and Insect Shield® Repellent, both of which repel mosquitos that may be infected with West Nile virus or malaria and ticks that may be carrying Lyme disease. Permethrin is the active ingredient in flower and vegetable insecticidal dusts, which can be used as a last resort. Refer to *www.pestproducts.com/insecticide_dusts.htm*.

There is no substitute for proper horticultural practices. Keep prevention in mind. Vegetable gardeners know that companion planting with strong smelling herbs and flowers keep many pests from attacking precious tomato plants and tender lettuces, etc. The chart of "Pest-deterrent miniatures" will help you to find plants to intermingle with the more defenseless plants, a kind of buddy system.

Finally, let's go back to the previous chapter on inviting critters into the railway and remember why we're gardening—to commune with nature, to find nature in ourselves, and to find companions within the plant and animal kingdoms to tell our stories. To put it another way, when you plant bearberry, expect to see bears. See photo.

16 Grass-like miniatures

1. Lee and Joan Sampson massed blue fescue (foreground) and sea pinks displaying springtime blooms.

Grasses and their look-alikes have a distinct artistic place in the miniature or alpine garden. In a landscape composed of little leaved trees and fluffy groundcover, the overall look can be cloud-like, fuzzy and frothy. Spiky, vertical grass blades, whether in a single clump or grouped en masse, break up that pattern, as in photo 1, and seem to tell a new story. Inserting grasses in the garden can also call attention to a change in habitat.

2. Japanese gardens show us how to efficiently create a simple water feature without water. Using imagination, the vertical, mica-encrusted boulder represents a waterfall. At the base, dwarf mondo grass represents the rushes found at water's edge.

3. Water features involve rock building. Trailing asparagus fern softens the hardscape, and stargrass, right, with its white star-like blooms takes advantage of splashes and boggy soil.

4. Water splashing off rocks causes the pump's reservoir to go down quickly, but water-loving fiber-optic grass comes to the rescue, catching drops and dripping them back into the pond on the author's Darjeeling Tea Lines.

5. When Jerry and Alison Ogden built their Possum Creek Railroad tunnel and 2'-high retaining wall, they found that Japanese blood grass quickly covered the man-made horizontal lines of the lumber and contrasted with the cascading woolly thyme.

Water feature borders

Here's the best habitat for grassy plants: near water. In full-scale landscapes, rushes, cattails, irises, bamboo, and tall weedy grasses bend over the water's edge, swaying with the wind. Like mini marshes, most of the mini grasses enjoy the bonus drinks they get living near water features. Mondo grass (photo 2) and sweet flag must have moist soil. Some like to live in the water, like stargrass (photo 3), dwarf papyrus, and

fiber optic grass (photo 4). See Chapter 10, "Aquatics have wet feet."

Because pondside 1:1 bulrushes stretch way over our human heads, some of the plants included in the following chart may be a bit longer than we might want in a strictly scale layout. After all, a 6"-long blade of grass is twice as tall as a 3" figure—a 6' human in ½" scale or 1:24—roughly the scale modeled in most garden railways. Here's the good news. Usually water

features are near the front of the garden for ease of maintenance and to show off bridges, so anything growing behind these larger leaves will look exceptionally small. It's all in the feel, a perceptual game. The willowy Japanese blood grass has red-tipped blades a bit too tall to put near buildings, but works nicely to screen man-made retaining walls (photo 5) and points to the scene above.

The chart of grass-like plants lists favorites found in garden railways.

16

Grass-like miniatures*

Common name	Botanical name	Size	Sun/shade	Description, comment	Zones
True grass family					
Variegated tuberous oat grass	*Arrhenatherum e.* ssp. *bulbosum* 'Variegatum'	1-2'	shade/pt.sh.	white striped, shear in summer when dormant	2-10
Bonsai dwarf tall fescue	*Festuca arundinacea*	2" cut	sun/pt. sh.	sod available, dark green turfgrass, mow it	4-8
Golden Toupee blue fescue	*Festuca glauca* 'Golden Toupee'	6-10"	sun/pt. sh.	golden blades with blue green at roots	4-9
Dwarf blue fescue	*Festuca g.* 'Sea Urchin' or 'Blue Boulder'	8"	sun/pt. sh.	steel blue tufts, divide every few years	4-9
Elijah Blue dwarf fescue	*Festuca ovina* var. *glauca* 'Elijah Blue'	6-12"	sun/pt. sh.	mounds make a blue sea when massed	4-10
Japanese blood grass	*Imperata cylindrica* 'Rubra'	12-18"	sun/pt. sh.	vertical blades topped by 3" red tips	6-9
Dwarf fernleaf bamboo	*Pleioblastus pygmaeus* var. *distichus*	10"	part shade	branching blades, cut back in spring	6-10
Korean grass	*Zoysia tenuifolia*	4-5"	sun/pt. sh.	no-mowing, mounds of fine light green blades	10-11
Alpine (rock garden) plants					
Thrift, Sea pink	*Armeria caespitosa* 'Victor Reiter'	4"	sun	soft blades in a crown, pink spring flowers	3-9
Thrift, Sea pink	*Armeria juniperifolia* 'Alba'	12"	sun	spiny blades in a crown, white spring flowers	3-9
Dwarf thrift	*Armeria maritima* 'Little Penny'	½"	sun	mat with stemless pink spring flowers	3-9
Red thrift, sea pink	*Armeria maritima* 'Rubrifolia'	4"	sun	burgundy crown, dark pink flowers	3-9
Clove pinks, pinks	*Dianthus myrtinervius* var. *caespitosus*	2-3"	sun/pt. sh.	light green mat, rose-pink spring flowers	3-9
Clove pinks, pinks	*Dianthis alpinus* 'Joan's Blood'	4"	sun/pt. sh.	glossy blades, magenta spring flowers	3-9
Day lily	*Hemerocallis* sp. 'Penny Earned'	8-10"	sun/pt. sh.	¼"-wide arcing leaves, 1¼" yellow flowers	3-9
Plantain lily	*Hosta* sp. 'Popo' or *H.* sp. 'Lemon Lime'	1"	shade	lavender fls, heart-shape leaves	3-9
Pygmy bitterroot, alpine lewisia	*Lewisia pygmaea, L. nevadensis*	2"	sun	pink (L. n. is white) flowers in spiky rosette	3-9
Dwarf mondo grass, lilyturf	*Ophiopogon japonica* 'Gyoko Ryu'	2"	shade/pt.sh.	dark green, tight clump, moist soil	7-10
Mondo grass, kyoto	*Ophiopogon japonicus* 'Kyoto Dwarf'	2"	shade/pt.sh.	dark green, tight clump, moist soil	7-10
Dwarf mondo grass, lilyturf	*Ophiopogon japonicus* 'Nana'	3"	shade	dark green, tight clump, moist soil	7-10
Australian astroturf	*Scleranthus biflorus*	1"	sun	very low almost mossy, light green	9-11
Dwarf blue-eyed grass	*Sisyrinchum idahoense* var. *bellum* 'Nana'	4"	sun/pt. sh.	clumps of stiff blades, blue spring flowers	7-11
Water/bog plants (see aquatics)					
Dwarf Japanese sweet flag	*Acorus gramineus* 'Ogon'	6-12"	shade/pt.sh.	yellow clumping iris-like leaves, moist soil/bog	6-9
Dwarf variegated sweet flag	*Acorus gramineus* 'Pusillus Minimus Aureus'	4-6"	sun/pt. sh.	yellow clumping iris-like leaves, moist soil/bog	5-11
Stargrass	*Dichromena colorata*	1-2'	sun/pt. sh.	white star at top, roots in water/bog	7-10
Miniature rush	*Eleocharis radicans*	1-2"	part sun	bog/water plant forming a green mat	6-10
Dwarf scouring rush, horsetail	*Equisetum scirpoides*	6-12"	sun/pt. sh.	non-invasive, in-scale rushes, water/bog plant	3-11
Dwarf papyrus	*Cyperus papyrus* 'King Tut,' or *C. p.* 'Nanus'	12-18"	sun/pt. sh.	18-inch high "palms"	9-11
Fiber-optic grass	*Scirpus cernuus,* syn. *Isolepa cernua*	12"	sun/pt. sh.	floppy blades drape or mound, bog plant	8-10
Dwarf cattail, dwarf bulrush	*Typha minima*	12-18"	sun/pt. sh.	narrow blades, brown "cattails," bog or water	3-10
Spring-blooming bulbs					
Chive	*Allium schoenoprasum*	12-18"	sun	oniony, edible floppy leaves, purple flowers	3-9
Dwarf leeks, fragrant onion	*Allium flavum minor*	6-8"	sun	soft thin tubular leaves, pale yellow flowers	3-9
Snow crocus	*Crocus sieberi* subsp. *sublimis* 'Tricolor'	4"	sun/pt. sh.	bulb with narrow blades, cup-like lily flowers	3-9
Snowdrop	*Galanthus nivalis*	5-8"	sun/pt. sh.	fine tubular blades, white flowers	2-9
Grape hyacinth	Muscari armeniacum, M. latifolium	5-8"	sun/pt. sh.	clumps of blades, white to blue flowers	2-9
Daffodils	*Narcissus bulbocodium* spp. 'Golden Bells'	8"	sun/pt. sh.	multiple heads from one bulb, floppy leaves	3-9
Starflower, red star	*Rhodohypoxis baurii*	5"	shade/pt.sh.	pink to red flowers, striped blades	7-10
Persian Pearl tulip	*Tulipa pulchella* 'Persian Pearl'	6"	sun	purple-red and yellow small cupped flowers	4-8

*Size is height; plants spread usually similar to height. Sun/pt. sh. =sun/part shade. Sun is five or more hours of direct sun per day.   Zones are USDA Hardiness Zones.

16

6. Richard Murray's many bridges and trestles create homes for dwarf horsetail (*Equisetum scirpoides* var. *contorta*).

7. Starflower blooms are big and showy, all the better to help us appreciate them. And those stripes!

8. Two shades of grape hyacinth (*Muscari neglectum* and the lighter *M.* 'Valerie Finnis') cheer up the hills in springtime. About the time the leaves get yellow and sad, the summer shrubbery takes over.

9. Even the shortest day lily is slightly too tall for landscaping the house, but here in front, it makes all the plantings in the distance perfectly realistic.

Massing the clumps of any tallish, grass-like plant, like blue fescue (photos 1 and 15) will spread out the clump so that it will be difficult to tell how tall the individual blades are. Should the hummocks begin to get dead centers, divide clumps periodically into three or four smaller "plugs." Pull out and recycle the dead straw-colored patches, then transplant the divisions in amended soil. This often brings the color back to faded grasses.

Dry wash edging
Knowing what we know about water features, the same goes for dry rivers of pebbles. We pretend the water just dried up two weeks ago. It will be back! The grasses growing at the dry creek's edge will hang on until then and continue to tell that story (photo 6). We humans need those dry riverbeds as walkways to maintain the trains and garden.

Sea pinks and fescues (photo 1), chives, clove pinks, and Australian astroturf are all drought resistant, once established. They take a bit of trampling if you use the dry wash for a pathway. Spring-blooming plants, like bulbs (photos 7 and 8), day lilies (photo 9), and dwarf bamboo (photo 10) have dormant periods brought on by winter. Korean velvetgrass (photo 11) turns straw colored during drought. Placing them near a dry wash will hide those traits. Here's one more praise of dry washes—if you need seasonal drainage, this pebble-lined swale will act as a floodplain and the roots will help to prevent erosion.

Lowly weeds
Grassy plants humbly serve the landscape. The shade-loving dwarf

10. In an Asian-themed railway, the 6"-high dwarf bamboo forests the tea house.

11. On the right in the intentionally poor soil of the gravelly road, Korean velvetgrass stays quite low.

12. The Shaina Japanese maple gets help in showing off its trunk from the 1"-high Popo hosta.

13. This shade lover gets tired mid summer and benefits from shearing when it goes dormant. Position variegated tuberous oat grass for spring and fall showing.

14. One might expect to find weedy grasses growing next to the outhouse, but the blue beauties belong to dwarf blue-eyed grass, a member of the iris family. Cousins have white or yellow flowers.

hosta (photo 12) helps by filling in under trees. Variegated tuberous oat grass (photo 13) lights up dark areas. Because the poor grass family is often cast as weeds among flowers, clumps of tiny blades, like dwarf blue-eyed grass (photo 14) and dwarf mondo grass (photo 15), can portray the odd neglected patch next to the barn, and along fences and roadsides. Speaking of interlopers, I sometimes leave inch-high lawn-grass seedlings (blown in or bird-planted) artistically positioned for photo ops while they are still in scale. But you know what they say … give them an inch …

Lawns, meadows and hayfields

Modeling lawns in front of little houses is probably best done with thymes and other micro groundcovers (see Chapter 18 for the chart "Low-down groundcovers"). For meadows with short spiky blades, warmer zones can use Australian astroturf (photo 16) and colder climates can choose from dwarf dianthus varieties (photo 17). If you live in Zones 4-8 or sometimes 9, where bonsai-type turfgrass winters over, then you may want to give it a try.

In my first railway for my grandson and me, I needed a comfy place in the middle of it where we could sprawl out

and play. I installed an area of bonsai turf sod, which served as a hay field in front of little farm buildings and as a biplane airfield. Even guests rested there as they wandered the various paths. I liked that the slow-growing lawn needed mowing only occasionally, which I did with a pair of battery-powered grass clippers or a string trimmer (messier cleanup). Maybe I should try golf-course, putting-green turf one day.

Here's a website for checking out low maintenance lawns from which to view your garden: *www.highcountrygardens. com/catalog/browse/native-turf-grasses/.*

16

15. Trash or treasure? Grasses, like blue fescue in front and dwarf mondo grass up against the rock wall, prove their value in Dart and Dot Rinefort's garden.

16. Lime-colored Australian astroturf contrasts nicely with the dark green trees, which may be slated for a ride to the sawmill on the Murray's appropriately named Green Hills Railroad.

17. Bob Stone of British Columbia chose a dwarf dianthus to mass on a hillside. Springtime will cover the meadow in flowers.

17 Junipers to appreciate

Richard and Melinda Murray's multi-trunk, variegated Japanese garden juniper has graced their yard for 35 years with its butter-yellow-splashed foliage. Now their Green Hills Railroad has a mature, bushy grove to shade the fishpond. Left of the bridge, the non-variegated variety, dwarf Japanese garden juniper, hugs the banks.

Junipers don't get much respect … at first. Wowed by showy flowers and striking colors, novices pass them by as nondescript, formless ramblers; hikers rein in their arms and legs to avoid the prickly leaves; new gardeners trot by in search of more glamorous beauties; but seasoned landscapers, having replaced those under-performing starlets, appreciate all that the genus *Juniperus* has to offer in its supporting role.

Jewel or juggernaut

Before condemning a juniper as untouchable, let's hear the evidence in its favor. Bearing the tiniest of leaves, scale-like or needly, it is the perfect "scale" plant to show off your railroad and other more statuesque trees, and it comes in a palette of colors, some of which display seasonal foliage color. The chart shows that they grow in all Zones except the Arctic. Give this genus sun and good drainage material, like sand or crushed lava rock incorporated into your soil, then stand back. Even rocky soil is okay. Junipers are drought, deer, and salt-resistant, and even foot traffic and pests rarely attack this rugged plant (once established). Bagworm and spider mites seem to be the worst pests during dry spells. Hose plants down to prevent infestation, but remember that too much water can rot them.

Sure, jungly junipers can reach the attic windows or spread from fence to fence, forming a no-man's land for snails and varmints, but tidier varieties are well suited for our railways. Let's critique four habits (silhouettes) in junipers we desire for railroads: a low, creeping groundcover, to model underbrush or green hills; a dwarf, multi-stemmed, upright bush that can be cleaned up to represent a grove of trees; a dwarf, upright, narrow spire of a tree; and, lastly, a full-scale shade canopy above our railways. Buy the right juniper and it will repay you in saved time as a long-lived player in your garden scenes. The chart lists some low- and slow-growing options.

Starting with the creeping junipers (photo 1), this young plant (less than two years old, bought in a one-gallon pot) has lateral branches that act as octopus "arms" to hug the rocks and hang over a retaining wall or slope. During the honeymoon years, we're happy to have their help in hiding masses of bare rock on hills and watercourses, or the mechanics of tunnel portals. Years later, we wonder where the water and tunnels have gone. You will find that the arms have become main branches with their own arms.

Jostling for space, old junipers (photo 2) overlap themselves and pile up unneeded branches, which you can eliminate. First, lift the tips, see that there's a perfectly good branch underneath, then cut off the new growth. Rather than clipping just the tips, which is a

1. On Mike and Holly Crane's Wasatch Falls, octopus-like branches reach out of the dwarf Japanese garden juniper to cover the steep rocky slope.

2. On Ronald and Justin Bregenzer's Fort Walt Railroad, blue rug juniper has carpeted the hillside for a decade and still stays tidy with judicious pruning. Silvery, berry-like cones are evidence of health. True to its name, this blue rug has soft, not scratchy, leaves.

3. A grove of young, unnamed juniper trees from one plant grace the Riggston Central Coast Railroad. Owner Dan Riggs reports he's "good with plants, not with names."

4. If you build your railway after growing shrub junipers for 35 years, you can follow Walt and Vee Permann's example. They resized a variety of large shrubs into trees for their El Dorado Lumber & Stone Valley Railrroad.

5. As a warning of a steep curve, the Murrays leave a derelict boxcar under the trestle, buried in 6" of shore juniper.

6. Rated for Zone 7, three dwarf Irish junipers, modeling a mini windbreak, show telltale but interesting defoliation and exposure of the trunk in the Pickett's Zone 9 railway.

quick fix that won't last long, cut away whole branches back to the "trunk." This technique will keep your groundcover nearer the ground to allow the trees and structures to stand out. As a bonus, weeds won't find the light of day.

Multi-stemmed junipers follow the same rules outlined in my article on clumping trees in October 2009 *GR*, *"Greening your railway: Clumping trees."* See links in appendix. Place your shrubby juniper (photo 3) where you can look through the trunks for added depth perception. Periodically clean off the sprouting growth from the trunks up to the desired branch height, maybe 3" to 8", and mulch lightly to show off the trunks. Now that you can see the start of individual "trees," separate them from the pack by clipping branches that grow toward the center. Repeat this process as necessary and give the heads of each tree a haircut to distinguish them from the mass of a bush. Get rid of unwanted trees at ground level and, *voilà*, a grove!

If you've been growing medium-sized shrubs for decades, you may not want to pull them out to build your railroad. You could clip away all growth from the bottom, minimize the number of trunks, then top them off into pom-poms (photo 4).

Ideally we will find some low, shrubby junipers, which we can let go to fill a need, like erosion control. When mature, the procumbent juniper, *J.p.* 'Green Mound', makes an excellent distant forest at the back of your railway. It hides the mechanics of your retaining walls and shows off the more tree-like specimens you plant in front. If you have an outside curve prone to runaway trains, plant a soft, spongy bed of shore juniper, as in photo 5. These junipers, while draped over a steep retaining wall, tend to hang, rather than billow out into thick bushes. Prune the ends or superfluous branches when necessary.

One more versatile shrub (see Sue Piper's section in "Ask the masters") is Loder's singleseed juniper, which, if planted in mass at the back of your railway, will form peaks that look like mountains.

Conversely, compressed (dwarf Irish) juniper, *J. communis* 'Compressa', models its sister, a narrowly columnar tree, the Italian cypress. No pruning is needed for many years, as this dwarf slowly grows, keeping its spire shape (photo 6). Live in the north? Hardier Pencil Point is for you.

Twenty dwarf junipers for garden railways

Common name	Botanical name	Mature height x width, description, exposure	Zone
Shimpaku juniper	*J. chinensis* 'Shimpaku'	3' x 6', blue green, slow, dwarf upright, spreading, sun/pt.sh.	3-9
Dwarf Irish juniper	*J. communis* 'Compressa'	3' x 6", green, narrow, upright column, sun	3-7
Green Carpet juniper	*J. communis* 'Green Carpet'	4-6" x 3', dark green, tidy, sun	2-6
Pencil Point juniper	*J. communis* 'Pencil Point'	4' x 1', steel-blue green, upright narrow column, sun	2-8
Shore juniper	*J. conferta*	1-2' x 6-9', blue green, flexible creeping, hanging, sun	5-9
Blue Pacific juniper	*J. conferta* 'Blue Pacific'	1' x 10', blue green, rapidly creeping, sun	6-9
Parson's juniper	*J. davurica* 'Parsonii'	2' x 5', blue green mound, salt okay, sun/part shade	4-11
Blue Pygmy juniper	*J. horizontalis* 'Blue Pygmy'	5" x 8", true miniature, tight mound, sun	2-8
Icee Blue juniper	*J. horizontalis* 'Icee Blue'	4" x 8', silver blue, creeping, sun	4-9
Lime Glow juniper	*J. horizontalis* 'Lime Glow'	18" x 4', feathery, electric green, vase shaped, sun	4-8
Mother Lode juniper	*J. horizontalis* 'Mother Lode'	4" x 6', golden-yellow green, sun to keep color	3-9
Pancake juniper	*J. horizontalis* 'Pancake'	2-3" x 2', blue green, flat as a . . . , sun	4-9
Blue rug juniper	*J. horizontalis* 'Wiltonii'	4-6" x 5-6', blue to purple, moderately slow creeper, sun	3-9
Japanese garden juniper	*J. procumbens* 'Nana'	12-18" x 4-6', blue-green, easy, creeping, sun/part shade	4-9
Greenmound juniper	*J.p.n.* 'Greenmound'	Almost identical to *J. p.* 'Nana' above	3-9
Variegated Jap. garden juniper	*J. procumbens* 'Variegata'	1-2' x 6-10', clear green with yellow splashes, sun for color	4-9
Buffalo juniper	*J. sabina* 'Buffalo'	12-15" x 5', bright green feathery mounds, sun	3-7
Blue Star juniper	*J. squamata* 'Blue Star'	3' x 4', steel blue, moderately spreading mound, sun/pt.sh.	4-10
Loder's singleseed juniper	*J. squamata* 'Loderi'	5' x 4', blue green, dense, upright column, sun	3-9
Grey Owl juniper	*J. virginiana* 'Grey Owl'	2+' x 4', silver gray, many berries, upright, mound, sun/pt.sh.	2-9
	J. = *Juniperus*	Size and color are determined in part by culture	

7. Modeling a mountainous Japanese village, Osaka & Orient Express trains pass under the dwarf Japanese garden juniper, trained by Jim Ditmer.

Ask the masters

Zones listed are USDA Hardiness Zones

Question: How have you used junipers in your railway?

Frank Lucas
Pleasant Hill, California, Zone 9
Once upon a time, we had a juniper hedge running the length of our red-wood retaining wall. When we had to replace the wall, a professional arborist pictured the hedge as a tree. He took out most of the plants but left three in the center and pruned accordingly. Now, 20 years later, it has turned out to be the perfect, shady setting for our little garden train. (See Frank Lucas's railway at *www.lcc-mb.com/CHUG.html*)

Ray Turner
San Jose, California, Zone 9
As I understand it, juniper is a subset of cypress (*Cupressus*). I planted a row of Italian cypress as a wind and view block on the windward side my railroad. These are about 10 years old now and about 15' high. I also have a *Cupressus sempervirens* planted on my railroad. This was supposed to be a miniature variety, but grew to 7'. I now have to prune it to 3-4' to keep it in scale. As you can see from the photo, the "scale" tree fits right in with the "prototypes."

[*Researching the difference between the genus* Juniperus *and the genus* Cupressus, *I find they are known in the botanical world as "sister genera." Because of their similarities, they're both members of the family* Cupressoideae. *The "dwarf" Italian cypress can be deceptively alluring when sold in a one-gallon pot, but it matures to 7', as Ray's has. If you want a miniature Italian cypress tree, easily kept at 2', you only have to look at its sister,* Juniperus communis *'Compressa', photo 6.*—N. Norris]

Kevin Ylvisaker
Mukwonago, Wisconsin, Zone 4B
Most of the junipers we use in the Rocky Lights Railroad are Blue Rug juniper. In only one case do we use it on the ground to spread, and this is in an area we needed

to cover without any other plant material. In all the other cases the junipers are trained as bridges and overpasses. We use ¼" hollow copper tubing to wrap around the main branch of the juniper, then curve it to form the bridge. So, a small plant is planted on one side of the track, then bare copper wire runs over the track until the plant grows large enough to form the full

bridge. To control the side branches, we use copper-colored aluminum wire, available from craft stores. As the plants mature, we trim all the side branches to keep the clearance for the trains and to keep the plant from looking too "weedy." We have about six of these in the railway right now and are currently working on one that goes over a small pond.

Cool shade from a clump of juniper trees affords guests a comfortable visit. *Norris photo*

The second columnar tree from the right is the dwarf form, compared to the regular-sized Italian cypress. *Ray Turner photo*

Sue Piper
Lakeside, California, Zone 10

Our favorite juniper is the *Juniperus squamata* 'Loderi', a dwarf, upright variety of the Flaky Bark juniper. It has delicate looking, green-blue compressed leaves, a relatively slow growth rate, and is tolerant of our Zone 10 climate. We have several that have been in our railroad for four or five years, and they have proven to be both disease and bug resistant. In addition to all of that, its best feature is its versatility. In its natural, upright-column shape, it makes a great forest tree. A little patience and simple snipping of the upward-growing tips of the branches will result in an unusual, graceful weeping tree that always draws the attention of visitors to our railroad. How often do we find a hardy, well-behaved, beautiful tree that can have two very different uses?

Two tunnel-bridges make railroading fun on Kevin Ylvisaker's Railroad. *Kevin Ylvisaker photo*

Narrow, upright foliage contrasts with weeping, full foliage, both from the same species on the Serusso Springs Railroad. Note flaking bark. *Sue Piper photos*

Getting back to the nightmare junipers, we can even find a use for them in the form of canopies above our railways. From a monstrous hedge juniper, identify the strongest trunk(s) and prune away side branches as you did with your multi-stemmed junipers. Let the top branches grow to create a shade tree you can walk under, as did Frank Lucas ("Ask the masters"). Evergreen junipers shed leaves year round, rather than all at once, but the leaves are tiny and scale like, and make a fine mulch.

To prune or not

Of the four habits in junipers, some types need pruning more than others. Anyone who wants a garden without pruning will have to let sections die back frequently and entirely rip out the dead growth. Of course, we're not looking for a weeding or pruning job, but knowing how plants grow helps us make wise choices. The rate of growth depends on how many years you want to go without pruning. Too much watering or fertilizing can speed growth and pruning, just as neglect produces dead plants in need of replacement. One way to get around pruning is to plant extremely slow-growing plants, such as Blue Pygmy and Green Carpet juniper and space them closely.

Japanese junipers

One of the easiest plants to establish in your well-drained, sunlit railway is juniper, and none more so than the dwarf Japanese garden juniper. In the October 2003 *GR*, Jack Verducci, in his article on *Juniperus procumbens* 'Nana', illustrated this creeper's many merits, along with versatility of placement. The Japanese have traditionally made good use of small spaces by pruning and the use of dwarf plants. Japanese gardens feature the cool use of (mostly) greens, texture, and massing to depict a reverence for nature. We railroaders like to spice things up. I've even seen a cascading *J. p.* 'Nana' trained over the track!

17

Resources

(See more nurseries in appendix)

FL: *www.royalcrestnurseries.com*
MI: *www.arrowheadalpines.com*
OR: *www.miniforest.com*
OR: *www.tinytreasuresnursery.com*
WA: *www.twogreenthumbs.com*

18 Low-down groundcovers

1. It seems this Elfin thyme has been groomed into a seamless, flat meadow. Not really—it just has the correct, sunny, well-drained conditions in Richard and Melinda Murray's Green Hills Railroad.

Locating moderately spreading groundcovers to serve as micro lawns, fields, and meadows can be harrowing. The grass can seem greener over the fence because, within each hardiness zone and within each garden, microclimates make some plants thrive and others struggle. If you wait a season or two, the thriving ones may undergo periodic problems while the slackers suddenly run rampant. That's a garden!

For example, our local hero, Elfin thyme (photo 1), filled in the farm from fence to fence in just one year. Then the tree overhead grew. In too much shade, Elfin and other thymes stretch in search of light and form bumpy hummocks. Depending on where the thyme is growing, a hilly effect can look fine. However, some gardeners prefer the small-leafed herb to grow flat so that farm fields, orchards, or lawns look realistic.

To achieve a horizontal appearance, plant thymes (and other sun lovers in the chart) so they receive five or more hours of sun a day. Don't over-feed or over-water your groundcovers, which would prevent slow, steady growth. Thymes and many alpine plants originating from mountainous climes thrive in gritty, poor, well-drained soil.

Prepare a platform

Why are we so fussy about low groundcovers? Primarily because the ground is the stage from which every other object in our miniature garden is measured. That floor is needed to balance the verticality of trees and structures—literally, to ground the scene. It keeps our interest cohesively glued from object to object. After spending considerable time clipping branches from the bottoms of little trees, it's nice if the groundcover doesn't obscure the tree's tapered trunk.

"How can I keep my mini lawn and pasture low?" is the number-one question concerning miniature gardens. It's been a puzzle for full-scale (1:1) landscaping, too. If you were to discover a groundcover that stayed small, with no mowing or maintenance, you'd be rich! The turfgrass industry has been trying for decades. Forty years ago, 4"-high zoysia, or Korean velvetgrass, seemed like a no-mow panacea until much of the state of New Jersey found that a harsh winter killed their exotic lawns. Even in warmer zones, zoysia inexplicably dies or goes dormant in patches but, if you can grow it, you won't have to mow it.

Next to the town's buildings in photo 2, the groundcovers are near unnoticeable. Effectively, they allow the stores to tell their tale of an era gone by. On closer inspection, the taller grass, zoysia, perfectly incorporated among the ledge rocks, suggests the area never was manicured and we wonder about the owner of

2. Paul and Renee Jacobs grow Korean velvetgrass and Corsican mint to keep other larger weeds out of town on their Saratoga Branch of the Colorado & Southern Railroad.

3. One winter, Jerry and Alison Ogden thought their Irish moss had gone away but it's coming back to the Possum Creek Railroad.

that business. In contrast, across the street, in front of the Mineral Belt Supply and the Dry Goods store, the ¼"-high Corsican mint looks like it's been stepped on recently, so there is life just behind those doors!

What we don't see is the landscaper/owner of the garden railway, who has to keep those low spreaders in check with

periodic scraping of the zoysia out of the gravel road and pouring boiling hot water on the Corsican mint to prevent it from overcoming the track roadbed.

All groundcovers have issues. The caretaker of the Irish-moss field in photo 3 was about to give up on this season's patchy growth when the low, grassy groundcover began to fill in again,

Low-down groundcovers*

Common name	Botanical name	Size	Sun/shade	Description, comment	Zones
New Zealand burr	*Acaena microphylla* 'Copper Carpet'	2"x24"	sun/pt. sh.	compact bronze foliage, red burrs	3-9
Greek yarrow	*Achillea ageratifolia* subsp. *aizoon*	4"x12"	pt. shade	ferny silver-green; low, flat, white flower clusters	3-9
Pussytoes	*Antennaria dioica*	2"x18"	sun	foliage mat with 6-12"-high fuzzy flowers	1-9
Corsican sandwort, micro lawn	*Arenaria balearica*	1"x12"	sun/pt. sh.	light green, thrives in poor but moist, soil	4-11
Tiny Green artemisia	*Artemisia viridis* 'Tiny Green'	2"x8"	sun/pt. sh.	small fragrant silver mounds	4-9
Miniature daisy	*Bellium minuta*	3"x24"	sun/pt. sh.	daisies bloom spring through summer	5-9
Living astroturf	*Bolax gummifera* 'Nana' syn. *Azorella* sp.	1"x6"	sun/pt. sh.	plastic texture, yellow flowers, dry soil	4-7
Brass buttons	*Cotula fallax*, syn. *C. lineariloba*	2"x12"	sun/pt. sh.	gray fluffy foliage, gold buttons, dry soil	5-10
Mini Kenilworth ivy	*Cymbalaria aequitriloba*	2"x18"	sh./pt. sh	mat, viny scallop-shaped leaves, purple flowers	6-10
Hardy African ice plant	*Delosperma nubigerum*, also *D. cooperi*	2"x24"	sun/pt. sh.	light green succulent leaves, yellow flowers	5-9
Cheddar pink	*Dianthus gratianopolitanus* 'Tiny Rubies'	2"x16"	sun	tidy mounds bloom spring to summer	4-9
Clove pinks, pinks	*Dianthus myrtinervius* var. *caespitosus*	2"x8"	sun/pt. sh.	light green mat, rose-pink spring flowers	3-9
Crowberry	*Empetrum nigrum*	4"x24"	sun/pt. sh.	evergreen, light green tiny leaves, black fruit	1-6
Wright's buckwheat	*Eriogonum wrightii subscaposum*	5"x18"	sun	gray mounds, look like ½" grass on a hill	5-10
Creeping fig	*Ficus pumila* 'Minima'	1"x6'	sun/shade	dark green heart-shaped leaves, fast growing vine	7-11
Spetchley English ivy	*Hedera helix* 'Spetchley'	1"x12"	sun/shade	tiny ivy vines, will creep up a trellis slowly	6-10
Green Carpet, rupturewort	*Herniaria glabra*, also *H.g.* 'Sea Foam'	1"x8"	sun/pt. sh.	flat green micro-lawn, white-stripe on *H.g.* 'S.F.'	5-9
Sheet moss	*Hypnum* sp. (hundreds of varieties)	1"x6'	sh./pt. sh.	true moss; moist, it's green; dormant, it's black	1-11
Pancake juniper	*Juniperus horizontalis* 'Pancake'	3"x10'	sun	blue green, woody stems, flat as a. . .	4-9
Miniature brass buttons	*Leptinella gruveri*, also *L. minor*	¼"x2'	sh./pt. sh	smallest brass buttons, gold button flowers	7-11
Silver brass buttons	*Leptinella purpusilla*	1"x12"	sun/pt. sh.	silver ferny leaves, yellow-green blooms	5-11
Platts Black brass buttons	*Leptinella squalida* 'Platts Black'	2"x30"	sh./pt. sh	bronzy black tiny "ferns," *L. purpurea* is similar	5-9
Miniature moneywort	*Lysimachia japonica* 'Minutissima'	2"x24"	sun/pt. sh.	lime-green mat with tiny yellow flowers	5-10
Creeping or spotted mazus	*Mazus radicans*	1"x30"	sun/shade	lowest mazus, brownish leaves, very moist soil	4-9
Corsican mint	*Mentha requienii*	¼"x3'	pt. sh.	paper-thin mat, purple tiniest flowers, minty	6-9
Dwarf mondo grass, lilyturf	*Ophiopogon japonica* 'Gyoko Ryu'	3"x18"	sh./pt. sh.	dark green, tight grassy clump, moist soil	7-10
Silver nailwort	*Paronychia kapela* ssp. *serpyllifolia*	1"x18"	sun	thyme-like, more xeric, gray with white flowers	4-8
Turkey tangle fogfruit	*Phyla nodiflora*	2"x24"	sun/pt. sh.	gray-green mat of oval leaves, ½"-pink flowers	8-10
Mini star creeper, isotoma	*Pratia pedunculata* 'County Park'	1"x24"	sun/pt. sh.	tiny leaves, star flowers, aggressive spreader	5-10
New Zealand scab plant	*Raoulia australis*	¼"x1'	sun	flat silver, slow growing	5-9
Irish moss, also scotch moss	*Sagina subulata*, also *S.s.* 'Aurea'	2"x12"	sun/pt. sh.	green carpet (scotch is yellow) micro lawn	5-10
Saxifrage	*Saxifraga* x *eudoxiana* 'Haagii'	1"x6"	sun/pt. sh.	mounds or cushions of rosettes, yellow flowers	3-8
Australian astroturf	*Scleranthus biflorus*	1"x3'	sun	very low, almost mossy, light green	9-11
Knawel cushion	*Scleranthus uniflorus*	1"x12"	sun/pt. sh.	light-green mat, tiny yellow flowers	5-10
Miniature stonecrop	*Sedum requieni*	1"x12"	sun/pt. sh.	green succulent mat, red in fall	3-10
Baby's tears	*Soleirolia soleirolii*, syn. *Helxine soleirolii*	1"x3'	shade	also *S.s.* 'Silver Queen', *S.s.* 'Aurea', moist soil	9-11
Woolly thyme	*Thymus pseudolanuginosus*	3"x24"	sun	trim off spent purple flowers, which turn gray	4-9
Elfin, also Minus thyme	*Thymus serpyllum* 'Elfin' also *T.s.* 'Minus'	2"x6"	sun/pt. sh.	lowest flat thyme, mounds in shade, glossy	4-9
Creeping speedwell	*Veronica oltensis*	1"x18"	sun/pt. sh.	azure-blue flowers early spring	4-9
Korean velvetgrass	*Zoysia tenuifolia*	4"x18"	sun/pt. sh.	no-mowing mounds of fine light green blades	10-11

*This list is not an exclusive representation of low groundcovers. For others, especially look for plants with the same genus as those listed, e.g. *Delosperma, Dianthus, Hypnum, Leptinella, Lysimachia, Mazus, Ophiopogon, Saxifraga, Sedum, Thymus,* and *Veronica*

syn. = synonymous name

Size is mature height by width (contingent on care, climate, etc.) after several seasons. Width dimensions are intended to show relative spread.

Sun/sh = sun or shade orientation; pt.sh. = part shade orientation, etc.

Zones listed are USDA Hardiness Zones

18

4. The Ogdens help the green carpet to creep away from the track. Note the boundary of mini boulders (left).

5. "If you take any longer to make that putt, this scotch moss will grow around us... and that bee at your left will think we're flowers!"

6. Crowberry, an evergreen mat of the tiniest leaves, produces black fruit. A modeling idea: plant it next to a bowling alley with the sign: "Pick your own bowling balls." *Ante Aikio photo*

7. Robin and Lucia Edmond bought natural tufa rocks and sunk them in the ground so that moisture wicks up to the native moss and a little mound of *Saxifraga* x 'Haagii'.

looking every bit the part of a country meadow in the wooded clearing. The same railway gardener had the opposite situation in photo 4, and lined his track with pebbles to ward off the creeper, named green carpet (*Herniaria* sp.).

Make do or do without

Even the best, lowest, slowest groundcovers gotta grow! Here are more ideas for coping but first, a secret: those perfect, seemingly flat groundcovers may be hiding the fact that they are uniformly matting several inches from the ground. We see only the top. To keep figures from toppling or drowning, it's a good idea to drill a hole and glue a brad or stiff wire into a leg. In photo 5, the golfers began life as hors d'oeuvres knives. On the day

of the photo I found them chest deep in a quicksand-like putting green. Rescuing them brought a bit of "grass" up around them for an amusing scene augmented by wildlife.

The theory of relativity, where mini-groundcovers are concerned, states that if it looks right, it is right. And yet, so many outdoor modelers fret needlessly, wanting it to look like the sprayed-on green sawdust one sees on indoor layouts.

Here's another trick. Where you want to model low, green cover near buildings, figures, or track, incorporate one-third or more sand or gravel into your soil around those areas to lessen the nutrients available for roots. This should stunt the growth. If that doesn't work, use compacted gravel soaked in glue water (one

part concrete-bonding adhesive to three parts water) and nothing will grow there for quite a while. Other fixes: put a plank or extra gravel under a sinking building when it gets buried; pull out groundcover by its roots around objects; or cut away chunks of the mat with a knife and transplant the divisions in bare spots. When groundcover gets too tall, it takes just a few minutes per square yard to shear it with battery-powered clippers.

Where'd ya get those creepers?

A groundcover website that has its own search engine to help you find just the right low plant for your needs, whether it be zone, soil, or sun conditions, is *www. jeeperscreepers.info.* You can search for plant use, such as pathway, wall, or lawn

18

Ask the masters

Zones listed are USDA Hardiness Zones

Question: In your experience as railroad gardeners, what are your most effective, yet easy-to-grow, low groundcovers?

On Cecil's railroad, the "grass" is *Lysimachia japonica* 'Minutissima'. *Cecil Easterday photo*

Cecil Easterday
Near Columbus Ohio, Zone 5

Lysimachia japonica 'Minutissima' is compact, about ½" high, has very tiny leaves, spreads but is not invasive (easy to pull out if it infringes on track space), does well in sun or partial shade, and doesn't mind drought. In early summer, it is covered with tiny yellow flowers. This is my favorite to use for turfgrass. Other plants that have grown well as groundcovers near buildings are *Ophiopogon japonicus* 'Nipon', *Sedum* 'Hispanica', *Leptinella* 'Platt's Black' (dark, almost black), and *Leptinella* minor (green). *Acaena microphylla* is aggressive but also great if you have the room for it to roam. A lot of the thymes work for grass or for fields. *Thymus praecox* will even grow in the shade. Creeping red thyme (*Thymus serpyllum coccineus*) needs full sun and has a fantastic bloom. [*Leptinella was formerly* Cotula. —*NN*]

Ray Turner
San Jose, California, Zone 9

I do like woolly thyme, but my favorite groundcover is Elfin thyme (*Thymus serpyllum* 'Elfin'). It grows and stays very low to the ground (typically ¼"). It has the tiniest leaves I've seen on any thyme and pretty purple flowers—very much in scale with the railroad. Thymes in general are hardy and easy to grow, which is nice for folks like me with a brown thumb. Look at *www.rainyside.com/*

Woolly thyme makes a pretty purple wildflower field in spring. To keep a low profile, spent flower heads should be shorn before they turn gray. *Ray Turner photo*

Frank is looking for a groundcover to replace the burned-out section of baby's tears over the tunnel. *Frank Lucas photo*

features/plant_gallery/herbs/Thymus_ Elfin.html. This web page discusses the culture of Elfin thyme.

Sue Piper
Near San Diego, California, Zone 10

Over the past several years I've tried every groundcover I could find that doesn't need a lot of shade to survive. I've planted mosses, including the terribly invasive baby's tears and the pesky, returning, spindly Irish and Scotch varieties. Of the many types of thyme, Elfin thyme is a favorite but is limited to certain areas due its mounding growth habit. Miniature rush is beautiful when first planted, but really does spread like wildfire and is extremely difficult to eliminate. Corsican mint and blue star creeper are also lovely but eventually overtake the area, track and all.

I've had the most success with the New Zealand brass buttons, of which there are several varieties available. Named for their golden button flowers, their leaves look like miniature ferns with actual mini "fronds." Purple brass buttons (*Leptinella purpurea*) has fronds about ½" to ¾" long that range in color from green to burgundy during the year. Miniature brass buttons (*L. gruveri*) has rich, lush green fronds only ⅛" to 3/16" long, perfect for mini greenscaping scenes, stays very low to the ground, and is easily contained by simply pinching

Shown are both the purple brass buttons and miniature brass buttons so you can see the size comparison. *Sue Piper photo*

back any stray runners. It may die back some in extremely hot or cold spells but always seems to come back denser and prettier than before.

Frank Lucas
Pleasant Hill, California, Zone 9

Baby tears was the first thing we planted four years ago. We used plugs and they filled in quickly, producing a nice, quiet, uncluttered effect.

They can be a little finicky. They need water and like shade. In the picture you can see how the plant is flourishing only on the left side, which is shaded by the fence. The area above the tunnel gets direct sun. I may have to re-plant that area.

replacement. After picking a plant, click on "More information" for growing conditions, larger photo, height, rate of spread, etc. It is handy to know that if I had to find miniature plants for interior Alaska's Zone 1, I could use crowberry (photo 6), a rugged mat I've seen growing on the rocky Maine coast. Specializing in rock-garden plants is *www.rockstarplants. com*, with an advanced search engine.

I identified a familiar plant online at Jeepers Creepers that is literally a weed in northern California. I've wanted to identify it for over 10 years—it's turkey tangle fogfruit (I kid you not). It makes a tough mat, flowering all summer, but I was afraid to try it in the railway garden because it had not been legitimized in print! Then I saw a listed plant that I know to be a wildflower in Maine, growing in lawns and meadows—mountain bluets, listed as 4-6" high—but I never saw the tiny blue flowers reach more than 2-3" high.

It's funny how a "weed" here or there makes an exotic "groundcover" somewhere else. It's also odd that USDA Hardiness Zones listed on various nursery websites or in garden books can be so contradictory. One will say "Zones 1 to 9" and another "Zones 5 to 8" for the same species. In Chart 1, the listed Zones have been double-checked but they come with no guarantees. Because of micro-climates and varied gardening practices, I suspect that zones are not intentionally misleading but represent successful gardeners' reports. Your local nursery should know what works in your area but may be limited in choices. If you garden on the edge of the listed Zones, protect that plant accordingly. For example, if you live in Zone 4 and buy a Zone 4-9 plant, know that you are gardening on the edge of its range.

Another website to try is *www.step ables.com* for 160 non-lawn groundcovers. I like to search at botanical gardens where labeled plants have wintered over for years. Online you can swap seeds at *www. alpinegardensociety.net*.

Some of us are lucky enough to have moss (photo 7). Blend scraped moss with buttermilk and spread your own. Or purchase true moss sheets and moss "milkshake" at *www.mossacres.com/products.asp*. Or just let nature change the moist, shady areas seasonally without effort.

19

Micro-miniature trees and shrubs

1. Paul and Renee Jacobs only occasionally shape their 10-year-old Hokkaido dwarf Chinese elm. Gorgeous corky bark, quarter-inch leaves, and only 14" in height make this specimen the perfect shade tree, just barely above the second-story window in the foreground.

Both new and experienced gardeners get perplexed when entering the wondrous world of miniature gardening. How to keep plants low is the biggest question, and starting your garden with the slowest-growing micro-plants may be the right answer. This chapter focuses on micro-trees and micro-shrubs, both conifers and broadleafed woody plants.

While working on an outdoor O-scale (1:48) railway project, it dawned on me that the plants near the track and buildings would need to stay in proportion to the trains, which are half the size of large-scale trains—pretty small. Even so-called dwarf trees can reach 6' in 10 years and require regular pruning to keep them somewhere in scale, preferably well under 2'. I was worried that O-scale trees might need twice as much pruning.

Not necessarily so—it turns out that specialty nurseries offer hundreds of varieties of little trees and woody shrubs that grow only an inch or so each year (photo 1). That's slow enough for any size railroad. On your large-scale line, wouldn't it be vacation-like to forego monthly clipping of those shrubs that obscure buildings that you'd like to show off?

Buyer beware

How do we know, when looking at a plant, what its growth habit will be? Young trees grown in tight pots can look deceptively dwarfish and especially attractive when they come with small price tags. I've been fooled by dozens of clearance "Christmas trees" priced to fly out the door. Although I've made them into interesting trees, I have had to stay interested and keep the pruning shears handy.

Now I check the other tag that comes with the plant and look for the words "dwarf" or "miniature," or (more accurately) a report of how many inches of growth can be expected in one year. The American Conifer Society has established standards:

Miniature plants grow less than 3" per year and mature to 2'-3' in 10 to 15 years.

Dwarf plants grow 3" to 6" per year and mature to 3'-6' in 10 to 15 years.

Intermediate plants grow 6" to 12" per year and mature to 6'-15' in 10 to 15 years.

Large plants grow more than 12" per year and mature to more than 15' in 10 to 15 years.

See chart 1 for a partial list of miniature conifers for every zone.

Many nurseries adapt these standards to also describe the growth rate of dwarf non-coniferous, broadleaf trees (photo 2), and woody, broadleaf shrubs (photo 3). If they state their standards in their catalog, we can be reasonably assured of a slow (and low) growth pattern. See chart 2 for a partial list

2. Late summer, little apples cling to Koshobai finetooth holly in Possum Creek Park, landscaped and maintained by Jerry and Alison Ogden.

3. The author found a small-scale ceramic building to make the mountain seem far away on her Darjeeling Tea Lines. The Kingsville boxwood shrub has never been touched by a cutting implement in 12 years, and remains only 3" high.

Chart 1 — Miniature conifers

Common Name	Botanical name	Size	Sun/shade	Description, comment	Zones
Dwarf balsam fir	*Abies balsamea nana*	12"x12"	sun	mound or trim for a tree, fragrant	3-8
Kosteri dwarf cypress	*Chamaecyparis obtusa 'Kosteri'*	3'x 2'	sun/part shade	fanned foliage, green cone	3-8
Tsukumo sawara cypress	*Chamaecyparis pisifera 'Tsukumo'*	8"x12"	sun/part shade	low green mound of fine foliage	3-8
Dwarf red cedar	*Chamaecyparis thyoides 'Meth's Dwarf'*	2'x1'	sun/part shade	classic forest tree	3-8
Tansu dwarf Japanese cedar	*Cryptomeria japonica 'Tansu'*	2'x2'	sun/part shade	broadly upright forest tree	6-10
Blue Star singleseed juniper	*Juniperus squamata 'Blue Star'*	1'x2'	sun/part shade	blue-green starry foliage	4-10
Little Gem dwarf spruce	*Picea abies 'Little Gem'*	10"x12"	sun/part shade	flat birdsnest	2-8
Jean's Dilly dwarf spruce	*Picea glauca 'Jean's Dilly'*	2'x 1'	sun/part shade	slender, conical forest tree	2-8
Dwarf black spruce	*Picea mariana 'Nana'*	10"x10"	sun/part shade	blue-green, compact shrub or tree	2-8
Blue Pearl dwarf Colorado spruce	*Picea pungens 'Blue Pearl'*	3'x3'	sun	silvery blue dense foliage	2~8
Bosnian pine	*Pinus leucodermis 'Compact Gem'*	2'x2'	sun	slow growing conical shrub or tree	6-8
Mops dwarf mountain pine	*Pinus mugo 'Mops'*	2'x2'	sun/part shade	spherical shrub, long needles	3-8
Sea Urchin dwarf pine	*Pinus strobus 'Sea Urchin'*	2'x2'	sun/part shade	low mound or prune as a tree	3-9
Tasmanian podocarp	*Podocarpus alpinus 'Red Tip'*	3'x3'	sun/shade	low mound or prune as a tree	7-10
Aurea Low Boy dwarf yew	*Taxus cuspidata 'Aurea Low Boy'*	2'x4'	sun	yellow ground hugger	5-7
Everlow dwarf yew	*Taxus x media 'Everlow'*	18"x4'	sun/shade	dark green spreading mound	4-7
Caespitosa dwarf arborvitae	*Thuya occidentalis 'Caespitosa'*	12"x15"	sun	fluffy green mound	2-7
Jervis dwarf Canadian hemlock	*Tsuga canadensis 'Jervis'*	14"x 7"	sun/shade	gnarled clusters of needles	4-9
Minuta dwarf Canadian hemlock	*Tsuga canadensis 'Minuta'*	6"x6"	sun/shade	dark green globe or prune as tree	4-8

Size is height x width in ten years, contingent on care, climate, etc. • Zones are USDA Hardiness Zones

4. Richard Murray has his little people maintain his little trees. Homer has pulled the Elfin thyme groundcover from around the stem of the dwarf Japanese Hinoki cypress.

of broadleaf trees and woody, broadleaf shrubs with the slowest growth rate.

What if labels get mixed up? If you need an exceptionally slow-growing plant, the space between branches will give away its growth rate. Little branches will be very close together, creating a dense, compact look. If those spaces (internodes) are more than 1"-2", then it is not slow.

When Ralph Moore, the grandfather of miniature rose growers, started hybridizing and selecting teeny-tiny roses growing less than an inch a year, some with 1" flowers, he called them micro-miniatures to distinguish them from true miniatures, which grow as high as three feet. Many a garden-railway farmhouse has been cheered with

Ask the masters

Zones listed are USDA Hardiness Zones

Question: In your experience, what are your most productive, most resilient, or easiest-to-grow "micro-miniature" plants? These would be true dwarfs that need almost no pruning and don't quickly overwhelm scale objects.

Low growing, truly micro-miniature roses line up left to right: Cinderella Gold, Little Pinky, and Baby Austin. *Peggy Friedman photo*

Cecil Easterday
Near Columbus, Ohio, Zone 5

For shrubs, my favorite is the dwarf littleleaf boxwood, *Buxus microphylla* var. *japonica* 'Morris Dwarf'. Mature size, reached in 8-10 years, is 8"-12" high x 12"-18" wide. It will take full sun but prefers shade, will tolerate dry soil if shaded, and grows in a compact mound without any pruning. The barberry's red of the *Berberis thunbergii* 'Bagatelle' and the *Berberis thunbergii* 'Crimson Pygmy' really make a statement in the landscape, are slow growers, and tolerate poor soil. I like *Pieris japonica* 'Little Heath', with its dainty, variegated leaves and bright, reddish-orange foliage on new growth. Another shrub I have used that is especially nice against a white building is the *Satureja spinosa*. It's a spiny subshrub, likes dry soil, and has tiny white flowers with a mature height of only 2"-3".

For taller trees, there are many choices. For a filtered airy appearance, the slow-growing *Chamaecyparis pisifera* 'Tsukumo' and *Chamaecyparis obtusa* 'Fernspray Gold' are good choices. Airy branches move nicely in the breeze, and the latter's yellow foliage is especially nice against the dark green of Alberta spruces, the slowest growing of which is *Picea glauca* 'Jean's Dilly'. Add the blue foliage of the *Juniperus squamata* 'Blue Star' and we have year-round contrast.

Dick Friedman
Sacramento, California, Zone 9

One day in mid March I stopped work on my train shed (nearing completion) to clear out and clean up a portion of

Cecil landscaped a replica of the house she grew up in, the Sparta House. The shrub on the right front of the house is a dwarf littleleaf boxwood. The trees on the left of the building are Little Princess spirea and Fernspray Gold false cypress. Dwarf spruce form the woods behind the house. *Cecil Easterday photo*

the railroad. I worked on the stand of micro-miniature roses, which divide the mainline from Magnolia Yard. Though the sun was bright, the air was still cool and the ground was still wet and cold (but it made for easy weed pulling). I first cut off spent gray canes (they will no longer bear flowers) at ground level to create more of a tree shape.

After that, I pruned the row of roses to resemble a windbreak row of trees (one to three stems each), such as I saw growing up surrounding the orchards of Ventura County. Then, I took a small amount of rose food (less than a tablespoon per plant) and worked it into the soil surrounding each rose plant and watered thoroughly. Even though the ground was moist, I gave the roses a good soaking. Five weeks later we enjoyed the micro-mini roses you see in the photo and we'll need to fertilize regularly for summer-long blooming. A couple

'Tis a *Serissa foetida* "Pink" (snow rose) on Frank's F&DLRR. *Frank Lucas photo*

of years ago, I stuck cuttings of these rose plants into the side of Red Mountain, and some of them grew.

[*Strip the leaves off the lower part of a 3-4" tip cutting and discard flowers before sticking into sandy, moist soil. Applying a rooting hormone on the root end helps.* —NN]

Frank Lucas
Pleasant Hill, California, Zone 9

When we planted our snow rose in July of 2007, we were a little hesitant to locate it in such a confined space. Here it is, almost three years later, and it continues to fit in nicely. It gets full morning sun, plenty of bright shade in the afternoon, and is watered by a dripper to keep its leaves dry. Fortunately, we have not had a hard freeze since then and we're keeping our fingers crossed on that one. We haven't had to prune it yet.

[*Serissas often sprout suckers from roots and require trimming at ground level to keep a single stem. Leaves are smelly, too.* —NN]

19

Chart 2—Miniature broadleaf, woody shrubs

Common Name	Botanical name	Size	Sun/shade	Description, comment	Winter	Zone
Dwarf Japanese maple	Acer palmatum 'Beni Hime'	3'x3'	sun/part shade	red smallest Jap. maple leaves	decid.	5-9
Bagatelle dwarf barberry	Berberis thunbergii 'Bagatelle'	12"x16"	sun/part shade	tight thorny shrub, red-purple foiage	decid.	4-8
Kingsville littleleaf boxwood	Buxus microphylla 'Kingsville Dwarf'	4"x6"	sun/part shade	tiniest, slowest boxwood, mound	evergr.	5-10
Morris Midget dwarf boxwood	Buxus microphylla 'Morris Midget'	12"x18"	sun/part shade	similar but lower than Morris Dwarf	evergr.	5-10
Foxii Nana dwarf heather	Calluna vulgaris 'Foxii Nana'	6"x12"	sun	tight green mound, mauve flowers	evergr.	4-8
Ghost tree, wire netting bush	Corokia cotoneaster 'Little Prince'	2'x2'	sun/shade	black zig-zag stems, ¼" leaves	decid.	4-10
Thymeleaf rockspray	Cotoneaster microphylla 'Thymifolia'	2'x2'	sun/part shade	prune to single stem "apple" tree	evergr.	4-9
Itsy Bitsy false heather	Cuphea hyssopifolia 'Monshi'	8"x18"	sun/part shade	shrubby, purple flowers	evergr.	9-11
Dwarf finetooth holly	Ilex serrata 'Koshobai'	1'x1'	sun/part shade	1" leaves, ⅛" red "cherry" tree	decid.	6-9
Kiwi Australian tea tree	Leptospermum scoparium 'Kiwi'	1'x1'	sun	dark red leaves, dark red flowers	evergr.	9-10
Little Heath Japanese andromeda	Pieris japonica 'Little Heath'	12"x18"	part shade	red new then white/green leaves	evergr.	5-9
Dwarf pomegranate	Punica granatum 'Nana Emperor'	18"x18"	sun/part shade	orange flowers, red 1½" fruit	decid.	7-10
Cinderella Gold miniature rose	Rosa x 'Cinderella Gold'	1'x1'	sun/part shade	multiple stems, yellow flowers	evergr.	4-10
Little Pinkie miniature rose	Rosa x 'Little Pinkie'	1'x1'	sun/part shade	multiple stems, double pink flowers	decid.	4-10
Cretan winter savory	Satureja spinosa	3"x5"	sun	spiny mound, white flowers	decid.	5-8
Snow rose	Serissa foetida	8"x8"	part shade	prune to single stem for tree shape	evergr.	9-11
Little Princess dwarf spirea	Spiraea nipponica 'Little Princess'	2'x3'	sun	dense mound, pink flowers	decid.	3-9
Hokkaido dwarf Chinese elm	Ulmus parvifolia 'Hokkaido'	18"x18"	sun/part shade	tiny leaves, big corky trunk	decid.	5-10
Lowbush blueberry	Vaccinium angustifolium laevifolium	6"x24"	sun	spreading with edible fruit	decid.	2-8

Size is height x width in 10 years, contingent on care, climate, etc. • Zones are USDA Hardiness Zones

micro-miniature roses, like *Rosa* x 'Tom Thumb' or the Chihuahua of roses, *Rosa* x 'Si'. (See Ask the Masters, Dick Friedman's, story on how he grows his tiny roses.)

Guarding your gems

Nurseries take time to select true, viable miniatures, create stock, and "nurse" them from the vegetative cutting stage to a substantially rooted plant, able to withstand the normal transplanting period. The extra years to achieve the size you want is reflected in the price.

Nursery people know the value of their products and want you to succeed in growing them, so they provide helpful information. They will tell you that small does not mean difficult. The dwarf varieties of the species are usually just as tough as the parents and sometimes more so. Your investment in micro-miniatures, price-wise, will be repaid year after low-maintenance year and won't need replacing because they've outgrown the garden.

As with conifers, each species of broadleaf woody plant has its own growing needs. Noting and providing the necessary conditions for the soil and its orientation to the sun will make it easier to keep your plant healthy.

Newly transplanted micro plants die mostly from drying out. Keeping the top few inches of soil moist is critical the first year or two until roots get established. Dig a deeper hole than the root ball and mix a small amount (about half the recommended amount) of fertilizer or amendment into the bottom of the hole, add more soil, then the plant, keeping its stem just slightly above soil level. Go easy on the fertilizer. Annual light feeding in spring should be adequate.

When you irrigate, do so thoroughly to allow the roots to reach down to the fertilized area. If you water shallowly and too

5. Tansu dwarf Japanese cedar looks right at home on the Murray's Green Hills Railway because they've been growing on the hillside for many years, unpruned. Australian astroturf greens the hills.

often, the roots won't need to stretch down. Deep (and wide) root systems withstand drought. Here's a tip I learned the hard way: conifers don't wilt like broadleaf plants—yellow needles indicate thirst, brown needles, imminent demise.

One trouble with these little guys is that they could disappear in the surrounding groundcover. Carefully trimming or pulling out groundcover away from the stem provides better air and irrigation flow, prevents competition for nutrients in the root zone, lessens moisture-born fungus on the stem, and you can see it better (photo 4). Instead of pruning, you'll need to clear around the stems once or twice a year. Alternatively, spread a shallow, fine mulch near micro-trees (photo 6), but not close to the stem.

Perspective pointers

Other than positioning micro-trees and shrubs next to buildings, figures, and smaller-scale trains, there's a valid reason for splurging on these easy-care, long-lasting plants. The most inaccessible area of the railway is often that mountaintop built from dangerously slippery or sharp-edged boulders. Even though it's just behind the town, we want it to look far away. Mass plantings of micro-miniature trees (photo 5) help to create the distance perspective if larger-leafed and tall plants grow in the foreground of the garden. It helps if the groundcover is super short, too.

6. Todd Williams runs only O-scale trains from inside to outside (note the three-rail track). He has found all the slow-growing plants he needs locally, including three dwarf Kosteri false cypress, here mulched with shredded bark. Blue spruce sedum in the background remains in scale.

19

i. Bibliography

All About Ground Covers. San Ramon, California: Ortho Books, Chevron Chemical Co. 1982.

American Bonsai Society [Organization providing information on tree pruning and care] www.absbonsai.org

American Horticultural Society, The: A-Z Encyclopedia of Garden Plants. New York: DK Publishing. 1996.

Ashberry, Anne. Miniature Trees and Shrubs. London: Nicolas Kaye Limited. 1958.

Atkinson, Dr. Robert E. The Complete Book of Groundcovers: Lawns you don't have to mow. New York: David McKay Co. 1970.

Bales, Susan Frutig. The Burpee American Gardening Series: Annuals. New York: Prentice Hall Gardening. 1991.

Bloom, Alan. Alpines for your garden. Chicago: Floraprint. 1981.

Conifer Society, The. [Association for the development, conservation, and propagation of conifers, with an emphasis on those that are dwarf or unusual] www.conifersociety.org

Dave's Garden [online gardening forum of gardeners, by gardeners, for gardeners lists USDA Hardiness Zones] http://davesgarden.com

Dwarf Conifers: a Handbook on Low and Slow-Growing Evergreens. Brooklyn: Brooklyn Botanic Garden Record, Vol. 21, No. 1. 1984.

Garden Railroading: Getting Started in the Hobby. Waukesha, Wisconsin: Kalmbach Books.

Garden Railways magazine. Waukesha, Wisconsin: Kalmbach Publishing Co. [for various articles see Links page in Appendix].

Garden Railway clubs and their websites is a link at the magazine's website: http://www.gardentrains.org/gta/community/clubs/clubs.asp

Gardening in Small Spaces. Mount Vernon, Virginia: The American Horticultural Society. 1982.

Hessayon, Dr. D.G. The Rock & Water Garden Expert. New York: Sterling Publishing Co. 1997.

Ishimoto, Tatsuo. The Art of Growing Miniature Trees, Plants and Landscapes. New York: Crown Publishers, Inc. 1958.

North American Rock Garden Society [encourages the study and cultivation of wildflowers among rocks] http://www.nargs.org

Schacht, William. Rock Gardens. New York: Universe Books. 1981.

Schenk, George. How to Plan, Establish and Maintain Rock Gardens, Menlo Park: Lane Book Co. 1966.

Stamets, Paul. Mycelium Running: How Mushrooms Can Help Save the World. Berkeley: Ten Speed Press. 2005.

Sunset Western Garden Book. Menlo Park: Sunset Publishing Corp. 1998.

Sunset Lawns and Groundcovers. Menlo Park: Lane Publishing Co. 1979.

Yanagisawa, Soen. Tray Landscapes – Bonkei and Bonseki. Tokyo: Japan Travel Bureau. 1956.

ii. Online sources

Go to www.gardenlines.net and click on the tab for *Miniature Garden Guidebook* Links where you'll find active links for the following subjects or organizations. You can click on the links for the subjects shown in bold italics below. They're organized as they appear in the book.

Introduction
27th National Garden Railway Convention near Kansas City, Kansas
28th National Garden Railway Convention near Chicago, Illinois

2. Zoning laws for climate compatibility
Arbor Day Foundation
Lookup tool for USDA Hardiness Zones
Canada's Hardiness Zones
Guide to plant hardiness zones

3. Design your mini garden
Garden Railways article:
Step up to terraces

4. Massing plants to frame a focal point *Garden Railways* article: ***Mystic Mountain Railroad***

5. Color me content
Architectural colors
Spring bulbs
Ray Turner's video of ***The Golden Gate Express***, hosted by Nancy Norris
Garden Railways article: ***Colorful annuals for the railway garden***
Garden Railways article: ***Regional gardening reports on annuals***
Garden Railways article: ***Early blooming perennials***

6. Easy access
Garden Railways article: ***An innovative indoor/outdoor 0-scale line***
Groundcovers you can walk on–Stepables

8. Prune trees
Chart for pruning evergreens
Bonsai Clubs International species care guide
Garden Railways article: ***Clumping trees***

9. Annuals for color
Garden Railways article: ***Colorful annuals for the railway garden***
Garden Railways article: ***Pathways: Regional gardening reports annuals***

10. Aquatics have wet feet
How barley straw controls algae
Online pond nursery
Minnesota Water Garden Society
Wayside Gardens

11. Cascading trees
ebook on bonsai
Blue Stripe Juniper picture
Schaefer Nursery

12. Deserts need succulents
Freeport, Maine's desert
Garden Railways article: ***Succulents***
Garden Railways article: ***Pathways: Cacti and succulents in the garden railway***
Living Desert in Palm Desert, Calif.

13. Drought-resistant plants
Native plant websites
Mediterranean climate gardening
High Country Gardens nursery
Garden Railways article: ***Drip irrigation: water conservation with a bonus***
Garden Railways article: ***Mulch for more than good looks***
Garden Railways article: ***Succulents***
Garden Railways article: ***Cacti and succulents in the garden railway***
Garden Railways article: ***Benefits of rock garden techniques***
Garden Railways article: ***Step up to terracing***
Arizona rainwater harvesting

14. Invite critters into your railway
Green prescription–Use the keyword "hummingbird" to search for nectar plants
Guide for butterfly host plants

Index of botanical plant names cross-referenced with common names for this book

iii. Online guides to miniature gardens to visit

You'll find two primary sources for finding miniature parks or outdoor dioramas of scale buildings planted with miniature plants.

Visit *Garden Railways* magazine's online link to public scale garden railroads. Go to www.GardenRailways.com and click on the "Permanent railroads you can visit" tab under "For beginners."

The *Garden Railways* list is updated online (regardless of the dates shown) as new gardens become available or cease to open their gates.

Also, be sure to visit the International Association of Miniature Parks, at its link: www.miniatureparks.org.

When planning trips to these areas, plan to visit these fun venues with your family. Many list contact information so you can research open dates and times.

In addition to the public parks, more and more nurseries that sell miniature plants are installing garden railways to show you ways to plant little trees and groundcovers.

iv. Online Nurseries, their USDA Hardiness Zones and contact info

Arrowhead Alpines, Fowlerville, MI, Zones 5-6
arrowheadalpines.com
Retail and mail-order nursery with display gardens. Specializes in rock garden plants, ferns, woodland wildflowers, conifers, trees, shrubs and perennials. Phone 517-223-3581

Blue Sterling Nursery, Bridgeton, NJ, Zone 7
www.bluesterling.com/Index.html
Wholesale-only nursery, carries more than 800 varieties of dwarf and unusual conifers. Website has directory of New Jersey retailers that sell the company's plants. The site is a well-illustrated compendium of dwarf and miniature evergreens. (800) 5-CONIFER

Classy Groundcovers, Blairsville, GA, Zone 7
classygroundcovers.com
Free shipping of groundcover plants. Online search engine. Fax: (443) 773-5627

Forestfarm, Williams, OR, Zone 8
www.forestfarm.com
Large online general-purpose nursery. Know the botanical name to search for miniature plants. Phone (541) 846-7269

High Country Gardens, Santa Fe, NM, Zones 6-7
www.highcountrygardens.com
Online and retail nursery and display gardens offer suitable plants for arid and mountainous areas, but also for xeriscaping. Phone (877) 811-2700

Jeepers Creepers, British Columbia and Ontario, Canada, Zones 3-7
www.jeeperscreepers.info
Use online search engine to find the plants and local nurseries that sell them. Phone (888) 258-3768.

John's Miniature Roses, St. Paul, OR, Zones 8-9
www.johnsminiatureroses.com
Online nursery with 175 miniature rose varieties,

4 micro-miniature rose varieties. Phone (800) 820-0465

Meehan's Miniatures, Rohrersville, MD, Zones 6-7
www.meehansminiatures.com
Mail-order nursery offers rare, miniature, bonsai and starter materials, as well as tropical and sub-tropical trees for indoors. Phone 301-432-2965

Mini Forests by Sky, Mulino, OR, Zones 8-9
www.miniforest.com
Mainly a mail-order nursery of miniature plants, visitors are welcome to the nursery and garden railroad. Call ahead for an appointment at (503) 632-3555

Miniature Bulbs, North Yorkshire England, Zones 7-9
www.miniaturebulbs.co.uk
Mainly features small-sized bulb plants; only ships to Europe

Moss Acres, Honesdale, PA, Zone 6
www.mossacres.com
Sells four kinds of moss, starter kits, and moss "milkshake." Phone (866) GET-MOSS

Nor'East Miniature Roses, CA, OR, WA, TN, Zones 6-10
www.noreast-miniroses.com/cgi-bin/nemr.cgi
Shows nurseries that offer micro-miniature roses from at least 4 nurseries

Rock Star Plants, British Columbia and Ontario, Canada, Zones 3-7
www.rockstarplants.com
Select rock garden plants with their online search engine to find the plant and local nurseries that sell them. Phone (888) 258-3768

Royal Crest Nurseries, Polk City, FL, Zone 9-10
www.royalcrestnurseries.com
"Pack and ship" as well as retail/wholesale sales nursery. Sells cold hardy palms and other sub-tropical trees and shrubs for Florida landscapes. Phone (863) 984-3000

Sandy Mush Herb Nursery, Leicester, NC, Zones 6-7
www.sandymushherbs.com
Mail-order online for scented geraniums, perennials, bonsai starters, wildflowers and their specialty of culinary and medicinal herbs. Phone (828) 683-2014

SmallPlants.com, Horseshoe, NC, Zones 6-7
smallplants.com
Online nursery with dwarf and small ornamentals of the species

Stepables, Salem, OR, Zones 8-9
www.stepables.com
Website identifies groundcovers (you can walk on) at retail stores or from their search engine. Phone (503) 581-8915

Sunshine Miniature Trees, Dallas, TX, Zone 8
www.sunshinebonsai.com
Buy bonsai starters and supplies, rare citrus trees or visit the retail nursery. Phone (800) 520-2401

Tiny Treasures Nursery, Salem, OR, Zones 8-9
www.tinytreasuresnursery.com
Mail-order nursery offers rare plants for rock gardens, miniature railroad gardens, plant collectors, bonsai, container gardening, trough gardening, etc. Submit orders by e-mail or phone: (503) 508-7878

Two Green Thumbs, Seattle, WA, Zone 8-9
www.twogreenthumbs.com
This online store of micro-miniature plants also offers little accessories, container kits, including micro-patio materials and has a blog. Phone (206) 352-0492.

The Violet Barn, Finger Lakes, NY
www.robsviolet.com/miniature_houseplants.htm
Miniature houseplants include African violets, English ivy, and begonias. Visit or buy online. Phone (585) 374-8592

v. Glossary

1:1 – literally 1'=1' or full scale, the "real" world.

½" scale – literally, ½" = 1', so that a 3" figure represents a 6' person, a 10"-long train models a 20'-long train, etc. The approximate scale of many garden railroads.

7.5" gauge – the distance between the rails on some ride-on railroads.

Amendment – any material, often organic (ex: leaf mold), which improves the soil structure in which it is blended.

Annual – a plant, which has a life of one season, usually blooming all season, bearing seeds, then dieing (ex: marigold).

Anti-transpirant – a liquid sprayed on leaves to prevent loss of moisture from leaves.

Apex – the terminal tip or top-most growing point of a plant.

Ballast – gravel used to work around railroad ties to anchor the track and prevent its shifting (ex: decomposed granite).

Biennial – a plant, which grows a rosette of leaves the first season/year then blooms, bears seeds, then dies the second season/year (ex: parsley).

Benchwork – a model railroad style raised off the ground on planks held up by posts.

Berm – a hill of soil, often to create a view break or sound barrier and change topography to be of more interest

Bonsai – literally in Japanese, a tree in a pot – an ancient art of cultivating trees in containers to appear old. In a garden, one uses bonsai techniques but plants the tree in the ground.

Boreal forest – the type of forest in the northern USA and southern Canada, in which conifers, mostly fir and spruce trees, become the dominant species.

Borrowed scenery – the real, full-scale scenery beyond a miniature garden, which looks in scale with the miniature garden.

Botanical name ¬ the scientific name in the Latin language that positively identifies a plant as different from any other. The first name is the genus (group) and the second word is the species (kind). Sometimes a third word or phrase identifies a variety of that species. English names in single quotes identify a cultivar (cultivated variety) of a species.

Canterra – a quarried stone formed from volcanic lava and ash that makes it light and carvable for troughs and containers.

Chinook winds – warm winter winds, which cause plants to start growing, then go away and leave plants to freeze.

Common name – vernacular name.

Compost – organic plant materials (ex: leaves), which have been allowed to decay so that nutrients become available to roots, when incorporated into the soil or on top as a mulch.

Conifer – a needle-leaved, cone-bearing shrub or tree, often evergreen (ex: spruce and pine), but also deciduous (ex: bald cypress).

Deadheading – removing spent (dead) flowers, either for appearance or to cause a plant, such as an annual or rose to produce more flowers.

Deciduous – refers to plants that lose all their leaves every autumn (ex: maple).

Decomposed granite – also D.G., crushed rock containing both small stones as well as fine dust, which allow the D.G. to set up like concrete when tamped and watered.

Directional pruning – trimming trees in a way that eliminates strong branches and allows weaker branches to change the overall shape of the tree, according to the artist's direction.

Dogbone layout – a loop of track, which has been pinched to roughly resemble a dog's bone. A bent dogbone is one in which the pinched area is bent into an L or U.

Dormancy – a period in an organisms life when growth all but stops, usually brought on by environmental conditions, such as cold or heat, so that the organism can conserve energy.

Drainage – the ability of water to percolate through soil is increased by the incorporation of sharp sand (more air pockets) into the soil.

Dressing – either improving the appearance of a landscape or the addition of attractive materials on top of the soil. Also, in fertility, the application of nutrients to the soil next to a plant, as in side dressing.

Dry wash – a narrow river-like swale filled with coarse pebbles to allow seasonal rain/runoff to drain. Also used as a pathway.

Dwarf – generically, a small or short plant and more specifically (Amer. Conifer Soc.), a shrub or tree, which grows between 3" and 6" per year.

Ericaceous – any lime-hating plant, which has acidic soil native to its habitat (ex: heather and azalea).

Evergreen – a tree or shrub, either conifer or broadleafed, which retains most of its leaves all year long, although it has "shedding" seasons.

Feather rock – a lightweight, porous natural volcanic rock used in miniature garden for mountains or hollowing out for containers.

Fines – crushed rock dust, which sets up as track ballast, miniature house foundation, or a walkway surface, but can be broken apart with a shovel.

Full scale – 1:1 (ex: the yard within which a miniature garden is built)

G scale – large scale or garden scale (originally from the German for large, grose), usually referring to the proportion of model trains to the original prototypes. G-scale is variable (ex: 1:29, 1: 22.5, 1:24 and 1:20). Most photos in this book show this scale.

Gauge – the distance or space between the inside of the track's rails, not referring to the size of trains (ex: for most G or large scale trains, Gauge 1 = 45mm)

Grade – the finished change in elevation, slope, or lack of slope in a landscape or railway. To grade a landscape is to change the topography.

Hardiness – the ability of a plant to survive cold temperatures, rated by USDA Hardiness Zones.

Hardscape – the non-plant structure, which holds the soil in place before planting

Hardware cloth – a flexible mesh of metal wire, often with ¼" or ½" squares.

Herbaceous – referring to perennial plants which die back to the ground each winter, then grow from the roots in the spring.

Humus – the decomposed organic matter, often from leaves and wood, found in soil and rich in water-soluble (available) nutrients and microorganisms.

Hypertufa – a mix of cement and aggregate, which sets up in a form to create a porous planting container, often a trough.

Inoculant – an amendment, usually a small amount of living organisms (ex: mychorrizae), which is incorporated into soil with a trowel or other implement.

Irrigation – applying water to a garden, whether with a hose, sprinkler or drip tubes.

Layout – a term for a model railroad, it's infrastructure and scenery.

Large scale – in model railroading, referring to the proportion of model trains to their prototypes (in the range of 1: 29 to 1:20) and synonymous with G-scale, more or less.

Microclimate – the changes in environmental temperature caused by natural or man-made land masses, buildings and varying exposures to the sun.

Micro-scale – referring generically to the smallest of a genre (ex: micro-miniature rose).

Mulch – organic (ex: bark) or inorganic material (ex: pebbles) applied to the surface of a garden to hold moisture, prevent weeds, forestall erosion, and improve appearance.

Penjing – literally in Chinese, a land-scape in a pot or tray. Miniature gardens use penjing principles, whether in a container or the ground.

Perennial – a plant, either woody or herbaceous, which lives from year to year.

Perlite – lightweight, white, expanded volcanic granules incorporated into soil to improve drainage. Also an ingredient in making hypertufa troughs.

Pinching back – the culture of cutting off the apex of a plant or tip of a branch to force new buds to sprout and grow a bushier plant or branch.

Planter box – a constructed raised garden with retaining walls of any height and any materials, whether commercial or natural stone.

Prototypical – referring to the original item (prototype), which is being modeled, usually in terms of actual size proportions, but also in likeness of detail, (ex: astroturf is prototypical of full-scale lawns)

PVC – Poly Vinyl Chloride, in irriga-tion, refers to hard white pipes for water conduits.

Raised bed – similar to a planter box and may have one side as part of a slope or hill.

Re-rail – to put derailed wheels back on the track so the train will run again.

Retaining wall – any type of construct-ed almost vertical wall (usually sloping 5-10%) for holding soil for a garden.

Runners – horizontal modified plant stems, which run just below or on top of the soil and root periodically to form new plants – a good reason to dig weeds instead of pulling them.

Scale – the proportion or ratio of a model compared to the model it represents. (ex: G-scale varies from 1/29th scale to 1/20th scale, or 1:29 to 1:20 compared to the prototype).

Starts – seedlings, cuttings or small divisions of new nursery plants ready for planting.

String trimmer – an electric or gas-powered engine that turns a plastic string rapidly to cut weeds.

Succulent – a plant or fleshy plant part that holds moisture and releases it to the plant during drought.

Symbiotic – referring to the relationship of one organism with another that benefits both (ex: mychorrizae fungus and a plant's feeder roots).

Taproot – a central root system from which most other roots develop. (ex: carrot)

Tender perennial – a plant that lives from year to year but is marginally hardy in a particular region, requiring special care, like mulch or wraps, to help it get through a winter.

Transplant – to shift a plant from a pot into the garden soil or from one part of the garden to another. Also refers to the plant moved.

Tree well – when raising the grade around existing trees, ideally create a well so that the soil remains the same height at the tree's drip line before and after. Many trees will survive a smaller well, as long as the area surrounding the trunk remains the same.

Trestle – a structure that supports road-bed or track across a span too long for a bridge.

Tufa – a naturally occurring, lightweight porous volcanic rock, used as planters, on which plants wick up moisture from the ground underneath the tufa.

USDA Hardiness Zone – a geographi-cally defined area in which a specific category of plant life is capable of grow-ing, as defined by climatic conditions, in-cluding its ability to withstand the average minimum temperatures of the zone.

Variegation – mutation of coloring on a leaf other than green, such as white or yellow blotches or edges. Often plants require full sun to retain variegation.

Vermiculite – natural, expanded, miner-al granules used to improve soil drainage, usually in nursery pots. Also an aggregate material used to make hypertufa troughs.

View block – any land mass, plant or structure, which temporarily blocks the viewer's ability to see all of a diorama or scene.

Watershed – the land and the runoff of water that feeds a body of water.

Weed abatement – a system of pre-venting and eliminating weeds.

Winter over – to survive a winter and begin sprouting in the spring

Witches broom – a compact, growth, denser than and growing on the parent plant. Many miniature trees and shrubs have been propagated from this type of tight growth.

Xeric – dry-loving plants which have fea-tures that allow them to live long periods without irrigation.

Xeriscape – to landscape using drought-tolerant plants.

ABOUT THE AUTHOR

Nancy Norris contributes the columns "Greening Your Railway" and "Plant Portraits" as well as feature articles for *Garden Railways* magazine. In addition, she's a garden railway planning and construction consultant, having founded her business, Garden Lines, in 1997 for building outdoor train layouts in her own San Francisco Bay area.

Nancy has a B.S. in Plant & Soil Sciences, a Master of Occupational Education, and has completed a full schedule of gardening in New England and California.

As an education researcher in the 1980s, Nancy became a ham radio operator and boat builder. She also learned to build and fly radio-controlled model airplanes, which her grandson wanted to fly. She gives him credit for towing her to a local train show where she saw her first copy of *Garden Railways* magazine. Now she and her grandson are active in their club, the Bay Area Garden Railway Society, building and running live steam locomotives.

AUTHOR'S ACKNOWLEDGEMENTS

My first thanks must go to my clients, who entrusted me with their yards and allowed me to expand my miniature gardening skills, plant selection and creativity to make an entirely new scene in every garden. Our local club, the Bay Area Garden Railway Society, gave me countless opportunities over the past 13 years to document their successes. Other clubs around the nation have opened their gardens at the National Garden Railway Conventions, as well as in Alberta, Canada. Railroad gardeners are some of the most gracious people I know.

The folks at Kalmbach, the hobby specialists, did a great job laying out this book. Special thanks go to Marc Horovitz for the historical slant in the foreword. My family has continually supported my hobby and business over the years, and without my husband, Ron's, advice, editing, and generosity, this book never would have come to fruition.

Garden railroading from every angle!

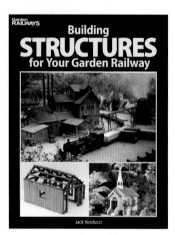

Building Structures for your Garden Railway

This book is the first comprehensive guide to cover everything you need to know about building structures that will stand up to the elements. Noted expert Jack Verducci shares his knowledge about researching, planning and drawing, selecting tools and materials, and construction.

#12457 • $21.95

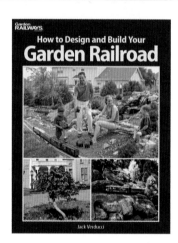

How to Design and Build your Garden Railroad

Increase your knowledge and skills with tips for designing, planning, and installing a layout; landscaping with natural materials; adding drama with structures, bridges, and trestles; and designing and installing water features.

#12406 • $21.95

Garden Railroading

This comprehensive collection of informative articles from *Garden Railways* magazine addresses the main topics of the hobby such as site considerations, developing a plan, landscaping, trackwork, power, and gardening.

#12217 • $22.95